PRAISE FOR MARK SAMUEL'S WORK

"The accountability workshop carried out with our leadership team has been critical in aligning the vision of each leader around self and employee empowerment, and it has allowed us to send a consistent and powerful message on what we expect from our people. My experience is that accountability is an extremely powerful tool to align an organization toward its objectives."

—Susan Gomez, director of human resources, Kellogg Corporation in Spain

"The concepts and methods taught in this book are practical and valuable for teenagers and anyone guiding teenagers to become future leaders and responsible citizens."

— Stu Semigran, president and cofounder, EduCare Foundation

"This book is easy to understand and gets your attention. The real life examples are effective in delivering the message on the tremendous power of personal accountability. At the Callaway Energy Center, we trained our leaders on personal accountability and used this book as a guide. This resulted in notable improvements in our teamwork, engagement, accountability, and performance. I highly recommend it."

—Fadi Diya, vice president, nuclear operations, Ameren Corporation

"This book, *Marking Yourself Indispensable*, goes beyond feel-good concepts. There are common-sense gems of applications intertwined with appropriate knowledge information to form wise transition points for healing. It is transformative, powerful, and practical."

—Gene D. Thin Elk, CEO, Medicine Wheel and Red Road Teachings

"This amazing book is absolutely invaluable and offers the reader so much more than a clear way to create job security and new opportunities at work. This book is about being and feeling your best in everything you do. It will change the work world and ultimately has the power to change families, habits, old patterns, and relationships of all kinds. Must read!"

—Dr. Jonathan Ellerby, CEO, Tao Wellness Center and Inspired Community;
author of the bestselling book, *Inspiration Deficit Disorder*

"Here at the University of Santa Monica it is essential that we provide a sacred and supportive educational environment within which each student can achieve significant and lasting personal and professional goals. I am pleased to see that Mark has put the principles and keys to paper that he has been using with our staff for over ten years to assist us in attaining and maintaining a high level of accountability."

—H. Ronald Hulnick, PhD., president, University of Santa Monica;
coauthor of *Loyalty to Your Soul: The Heart of Spiritual Psychology*

"When people leave our leadership workshop, they are on fire to create a high performance workplace. Once they return to work, they encounter the same traditional work culture they left the week before. Embracing Mark's approach to accountability creates a confidence and freedom to overcome obstacles versus being overwhelmed by them. Mark's wisdom is a gift; we share that gift with all our clients."

—Sue Bingham, founder, HPWP Consulting,

"Mark's book, *Making Yourself Indispensable*, provides a road map to living a fulfilling life both at home and at work. Mark's book gives clear, practical instructions to help the reader take control of their life in a way that also opens their heart, which is essential to building the human spirit. It is truly inspiring!"

—Agapi Stassinopoulos, author of *Unbinding the Heart: A Dose of Greek Wisdom, Generosity and Unconditional Love*

"Applying the personal Accountability model in our center we were able to respond to this challenging time of tough regulations. We implement new behaviors through all levels of the organization that were not negotiable and these were aligned to our key performance indicators. We are still searching for excellence and we are so pleased to have installed this model in our culture"

—Gisela Perozo, HR director, Maracay Medical Center in Venezuela

"Mark Samuel has written such a clear and practical book on how to make oneself indispensable. The gift of this book is the ability to adapt the processes to our own lives and walk away with measured steps to take and apply to any situation, which is truly empowering. *Making Yourself Indispensable* made me aware of my hidden imperfections, my strengths, and my "purpose-driven" career on a deeper level. This is a book I will use again and again. Thank you, Mark Samuel!"

—Philip Barr, MD, medical director, Pinnacle Care

"Mark Samuel has written an insightful and very practical book that is not just about personal accountability but also about what accountability will help us achieve: "indispensability." Samuel has made an extremely valuable contribution to our understanding of accountability and to our quest for the kind of successful life/career that has true accountability at its core."

—Steven Daniel, Ph.D., director of program planning, The Institute for Management Studies

"So what really makes an employee high potential? In very pragmatic terms Mark Samuel relates how it is not enough to be a subject-matter expert or perform to a list of leadership core competencies. Regardless of the complexity around us or the briskness of the winds of change that may attempt to drive us off course, taking initiative, being consistent and having others count on us to do what we say will we do—true acCOUNTability—sets people apart—particularly if we intend to make the most of what we do, and who we ARE, in service to others."

—Dr. Zara F. Larsen, change leadership consultant and coach, host of *Circles of Change* radio program

"Accountability is a key concept in moving an organization forward, especially in a challenging business climate. The principles and practices expressed in *Making Yourself Indispensible* provide a clear, concise pathway for easy and efficient application in today's competitive business environment. Of equal significance is the manner in which the author demonstrates how these same principles, when applied to one's personal life, can enhance one's sense of gratification and achievement, contributing to their professional life."

—Cindy Tucker, Americas' senior customer contact and business center manager, Agilent Technologies

"The personal accountability model allowed us to build a clear vision of excellence for our future and gave us the opportunity to define our path of success. It was understood for all levels of the company. Our new habits of execution and priorities brought about our expected results. Our focus was the human factor and his motivation toward better interaction and execution. I am convinced that the Personal Accountability Model was the best way to achieve outstanding results."

—Juan Seijas, plant manager, Empresas Polar

"Making Yourself Indispensable is a practical guide to living your life with integrity and commitment at home and at work. The topics and exercises encourage introspection and practical solutions using real life examples. Everyone needs to regain perspective from time to time and this book can help people do just that!"

—Mary Ann Sutherland, vice president, human resources, DST Output

"The principles presented through Accountability Based Leadership have proven their impact over the twenty plus years I have been in human resources and learning and development. The concepts can be applied in a variety of ways. From a personal perspective, I have relied on these concepts to clarify my intentions and guide my leadership effectiveness with others. In my role as a development professional, I have witnessed the positive impact these concepts can have on team effectiveness through increased personal accountability, team commitment, and a culture that encourages quick, effective resolution of issues or breakdowns."

—David Sanders, director of learning and development, Old Navy Stores

PRAISE FOR MARK SAMUEL'S PREVIOUS WORK:

"An inspirational and practical guide for self-improvement. I recommend it to anyone who wants to become the CEO of their own life."

—Ken Blanchard, coauthor, *The One Minute Manager* and *The Leadership Pill*.

"I played for one remarkable team and for one great city almost all of my baseball career and I have been so blessed. What can I say about this inspirational book? It supports what I've always believed: The commitments we make and keep to ourselves and the people in our lives are the key to achieving our genuine dreams."

—Ernie Banks, "Mr.Cub," Baseball Hall of Famer, 512 career home run hitter

"An empowering book that provides tough-minded strategies for avoiding the trap of victimhood and becoming the hero of your own life."

—Elizabeth Forsythe Hailey, author, *A Woman of Independent Means*

"A fire officer lives and breathes accountability to his superiors, the men under his command who dare to go with him into the most dangerous situations, and his community. Most of all, he is accountable to himself for his decisions. Without accountability, there is no fire service. Let this book be an inspiration and direction for you to move forward in your life bravely and purposefully."

—Lieutenant David Kahn, New York City Fire Department, retired

"The first step to creating a wealthy life is starting from wherever you are today. That self-honesty takes the highest level of personal accountability. Mark and Sophie's book assists us in moving past the judgments that often keep us stuck in limitation, freeing us to experience a life of prosperity and abundance."

—Loral Langemeier, president, founder, Live Out Loud

MAKING YOURSELF
INDISPENSABLE

MAKING YOURSELF INDISPENSABLE

THE POWER *of* PERSONAL ACCOUNTABILITY

MARK SAMUEL

Portfolio / Penguin

PORTFOLIO / PENGUIN
Published by the Penguin Group
Penguin Group (USA) Inc., 375 Hudson Street,
New York, New York 10014, U.S.A.
Penguin Group (Canada), 90 Eglinton Avenue East, Suite 700,
Toronto, Ontario, Canada M4P 2Y3
(a division of Pearson Penguin Canada Inc.)
Penguin Books Ltd, 80 Strand, London WC2R 0RL, England
Penguin Ireland, 25 St. Stephen's Green, Dublin 2, Ireland
(a division of Penguin Books Ltd)
Penguin Books Australia Ltd, 250 Camberwell Road, Camberwell,
Victoria 3124, Australia
(a division of Pearson Australia Group Pty Ltd)
Penguin Books India Pvt Ltd, 11 Community Centre, Panchsheel Park,
New Delhi—110 017, India
Penguin Group (NZ), 67 Apollo Drive, Rosedale, Auckland 0632,
New Zealand (a division of Pearson New Zealand Ltd)
Penguin Books (South Africa) (Pty) Ltd, 24 Sturdee Avenue,
Rosebank, Johannesburg 2196, South Africa

Penguin Books Ltd, Registered Offices:
80 Strand, London WC2R 0RL, England

First published in 2012 by Portfolio / Penguin,
a member of Penguin Group (USA) Inc.

10   9   8   7   6

Library of Congress Cataloging-in-Publication Data

Samuel, Mark, 1954–
    Making yourself indispensable : the power of personal accountability / Mark Samuel.
        p. cm.
    Includes index.
    ISBN 978-1-59184-469-3
    1. Success in business.   2. Self-management (Psychology)   3. Responsibility.   I. Title.
    HF5386.S322 2012
    650.1—dc23   2011045716

Printed in the United States of America
Set in Sabon LT Std
Designed by Spring Hoteling

CONTENTS

Foreword ix

Introduction 1

CHAPTER ONE 9
Committing to Make Yourself Indispensable

CHAPTER TWO 41
The Road Map

CHAPTER THREE 50
The Victim Loop

CHAPTER FOUR 69
Intention: Take Charge of Your Life

CHAPTER FIVE 86
Recognize Your Current Reality

CHAPTER SIX 99
The Power of Taking Ownership

CHAPTER SEVEN 117
Gaining Strength Through Forgiveness

CHAPTER EIGHT 137
Self-Examination to Foster Solutions

CHAPTER NINE 152
Master Learner—Your Default Response

CHAPTER TEN 170
Take Action to Be Successful

CHAPTER ELEVEN 189
The Missing Step—Celebrating Success

CHAPTER TWELVE 198
Living an Indispensable Life

Acknowledgments 213

References 215

Index 217

FOREWORD

Self-management and its correlation with professional success have been recognized and extolled for at least a hundred years. Early classics educated us on how to win friends and influence people (Dale Carnegie) and prescribed behaviors for being an effective executive (Peter Drucker). The latter's seminal thinking and writing, making us aware of the cognitive and interactive capabilities required for a new world of "knowledge work" (versus purely manual skills for making and moving things), was a harbinger of a new field, continually expanding in breadth and depth and now categorized as an "industry": executive, management, and professional development.

How we are who we are can make a transformational difference in our jobs, careers, and lives; and that's something that can be learned and practiced—not simply something we innately possess.

Awareness of the link between improvements in personal effectiveness and accelerated results grew exponentially in the 1970s and 1980s, as the explosion of the personal-growth-training movement paralleled the birth of and rapid advancements in the field of organizational development. Some of us remember with nostalgia old hippies meeting with U.S. Army researchers, exploring how love might make a more effective military.

Things have progressed. We've sandpapered away a lot of the fluff, romanticism, and craziness that characterized earlier attempts at that fusion of results orientation and touchy-feeliness. Those of us who've been involved in both camps have gotten older and smarter, enduring real-life challenges that put all that noble-sounding stuff to the test.

To be very fair, much awareness and learning out of that heady time of self-development exploration has proven its validity in spades. And in the following pages Mark Samuel has done a superb job of "bringing up the rear" for us—distilling and synthesizing tested models for improving our odds in life and work. His particular focus on applying the personal accountability factor in significantly improving team performance over many years provides a resource and depth of experience for us.

Herein are the spot-on principles for ensuring your perceived value in the world that matters to you. I can personally attest to their relevance and validity in my own life and work. This book provides plenty of real-life examples of how these dynamics play out, making them easy to relate to. And what I particularly love about Mark's work is the integrity in his approach and expression. He talks about humility with humility and courage with courage. His keys to successfully traversing the slings and arrows of our outrageous fortunes are validated by his own stories of missteps and corrections. This is a rich reminder of core truths about our effectiveness and self-esteem and that we're all in this ongoing game together.

David Allen, author of *Getting Things Done:*
The Art of Stress-Free Productivity
November 2011
Santa Barbara, California

INTRODUCTION

Imagine waking up in the morning and looking forward to your day. You are enthusiastic about going to work. You are valued by your boss and praised regularly for your contributions to your customers, the organization, and your team. People come to you with questions, problems, and needs for more information because you either have the answers or know where to get them. Why? Because you are trusted, keep your commitments, and achieve what needs to be done. And you are easy to talk to without the "ego" walls that other high achievers put up. You are the "go to" person people dream of having on their team. You are not only highly successful in your current job but are being developed for your next promotion and pay raise. You feel a sense of control and security, because even though jobs can be eliminated, you are such a high value to the organization that it will do whatever possible to retain you. And if it can't, you will have no trouble getting a new job, due to the value you create and connections you have developed based on the "goodwill" you have established along the way. Most important, when you go home at the end of your work-day, you feel optimistic, energized, and at peace because it was another day where you received praise from those around you. In fact, the good feelings continue when you enter your home, as you create the same sense of admiration and appreciation with your family and friends that you do with your coworkers. You have a wonderful balance between your personal and your work life. You feel fulfilled and satisfied with your life.

By now you might be saying to yourself, "This doesn't happen in the real world. In my world, jobs around me have been lost and my workload has increased. Everything is 'priority number one' in my organization, and I don't have the time to get everything done. I don't have time to help or serve others with so many responsibilities to complete. And what makes this worse is that success feels like a moving target. One day success is defined by meeting productivity goals. The next day success is defined by slowing down to ensure high quality standards. Then success is more about meeting safety procedures. As soon as I am clear about one direction, it changes. I feel completely out of control. By the end of the day, I not only feel burned out and beat up but am exhausted and don't have time for my family or a personal life. I am left worried about what the next day has in store."

This book is a "road map" for dealing with the tough realities of current working conditions and experiencing the uplifting sense of confidence and well-being described in the first paragraph. You will be given many jewels of insight and tools for achieving the highest level of success and satisfaction from your life at work that will translate to your personal life. Even more valuable, you will have a clear, step-by-step process for overcoming challenges and obstacles that currently bring you down or result in extra stress. You will take those challenges and, using the road map provided in this book, transform those into your stepping-stones to achieving greater results. While this book is inspirational, it is not a "feel-good" book based on affirming how wonderful you already are. This book provides practical tools for taking action, getting results, and achieving your goals and aspirations. Yes, you will "feel good," but as a result of accomplishing your goals. This is not a book based on theory or one person's approach to success. The Personal Accountability Model is a road map, and the set of tools provided in this book have been used by thousands of people around the world since 1986, when this model and process were first designed. This book was first published in 2004 but has been completely updated with several new chapters and content added to old chapters, including new concepts, keys for success, traps to avoid, and exercises to make this information come alive for you. In addition, *Making Yourself Indispensable* contains many experiences and stories of others who came before you, and responds to the most recent trends in the world we live in today. So the good news is that the Personal Accountability Model and road map have assisted others in achieving sustained results and helped them to adapt to change. In other words, the tools and processes taught in this book are proven to achieve sustainable success regardless of the changes and obstacles thrown at us.

FEELING OUT OF CONTROL

Feeling dispensable is nothing less than discouraging, depressing, and hopeless. No matter how hard we try and no matter how hard we work, nothing is good enough. Even getting good results is not good enough when you feel dispensable. Feeling dispensable comes from the experience of being disposable, replaceable, unnecessary, or redundant. In fact, when there is a large talent pool in an organization, you might hear a manager claim, "If you don't like it here, you can be replaced." And we can feel this way at work, with our family, and even by ourselves. In any of these situations, we can feel unsafe, helpless, and out of control. At work we are threatened by the feeling that we could be fired or lose our job without protection. And we have learned through recent events that even job security based on being part of a union or in a government job is not enough to keep us safe. Who protects us when the company we work for sells us off or goes out of business? It's scary, it's frustrating, and it's demoralizing. But there's hope even in the worst of circumstances; you can make yourself indispensable—and experience the confidence, positive energy, and success that come from taking the steps in this book.

MAKING YOURSELF DISPENSABLE

Many people blame their dispensability on the bad economy, the unfair organization they work for, the unreasonable boss, the lack of resources, their insensitive spouse, their ungrateful children, or

their poor "lot in life" given the poor conditions of their upbringing—
yes, at the end of the day it is their parents' fault. Since we can't
control our environment, of course we are dispensable. This is
further reinforced when organizations claim that no one is indispensable. So why even try? And therein lies the trap, or should
I say quicksand.

Apart from someone else taking your life, no one can make
you dispensable but you. There are ten behaviors that foster dispensability:

- Saying you will do something and not doing it—ever

- Committing to do something on time and missing the
  due date—without letting people know ahead of time

- Not letting others know when there is a problem or
  you need help, causing a crisis for everyone

- Blaming others (teammates, other departments, or family members) when things go wrong

- Voicing complaints (repeatedly) without offering or
  participating in finding solutions

- Being the naysayer when changes are discussed and
  resisting anything new

- Focusing on your personal success at the expense or
  exclusion of others

- Settling for mediocrity in your performance, teamwork, or communication

- Not apologizing or taking ownership when you make
  a mistake, and thus not learning from it either

- Expecting to be rewarded or promoted just for showing
  up to work without demonstrating high performance,
  or thinking you're the best when you aren't

At the core, each of these behaviors creates mistrust. In other words, no one can depend on you. You have made yourself useless. No one can feel safe with you, and you have become a liability. And you certainly won't be contributing to achieving successful results or an effective and safe organization.

DON'T BE FOOLED

If you are at the top of your game—a top performer with a history of promotions—you could still be at risk of being dispensable. Why? Because becoming indispensable is a process, not an event.

One of the most disheartening situations I ever experienced as a consultant took place at a medical center embarking on a major culture change to increase the cross-functional collaboration and leadership at the middle-management level. Of sixteen middle managers only three people had the consciousness for such a shift. (The rest demonstrated silo behavior, viewing departmental gains as more important than what was best for the organization as a whole.) One of these three middle managers was Sue. She was viewed as a mentor by many of the other middle managers, so she was tasked with leading the change effort. The culture change not only was successful but led the organization in achieving awards in its industry for patient satisfaction, high performance standards, and high morale. And it wouldn't have been successful without Sue's leadership. However, five years later Sue found herself struggling to keep her job. How could that be? While the organization's culture and performance grew through greater collaboration and commitment, Sue stopped growing. Being so far ahead of everyone else based on her past results, she failed to continue developing her leadership and technical skills. She got comfortable being the top middle manager in her organization. But others improved due to the culture change. So much so that Sue's relative performance became insufficient to maintain her position. She went from indispensable to dispensable.

THE ROAD MAP FOR MAKING YOURSELF INDISPENSABLE

No matter whether you have felt dispensable up until now and want to become indispensable or are at the top of your game and want to stay there, this book is your road map to success. The first chapter gives an in-depth look at what it means to be indispensable, avoiding the traps that cause "hollow" indispensability and leave people vulnerable and surprised when their world falls apart. More important, you will leave chapter 1 with six key choices for making yourself indispensable. Then in chapter 2 you will be guided through the road map to becoming indispensable, so that you are completely set up for success. You will learn how to prevent the six ways people sabotage their success in chapter 3.

In chapter 4 you will take the first step on your path to becoming indispensable by clarifying your picture of success—taking a good look at exactly what is important to you—your dreams and the goals to which you want to be indispensable. At the end of the day, you want to make yourself indispensable to your own aspirations. Then you know you will be not only successful but happy in your success. This book doesn't advocate giving up on enjoying your life to make yourself indispensable—that is never sustainable. So it is critical to clearly understand your optimal balance among work, family, play, and personal or spiritual goals.

As human beings we experience mistakes, mishaps, and failings. That is normal, and no matter how great you become, you will still have your off moments. It is important to integrate the lessons from those failings into your playbook and to acknowledge those negative feelings, like frustration and discouragement, but do not wallow in them. You won't be perfect in your actions, behaviors, or communication, but that need not stop you from making yourself indispensable. Everyone has their shortcomings, and in chapter 5 you will have a chance to explore the particular traps that have sabotaged you in the past, so you can take dominion over those negative aspects of your makeup. This is most people's favorite chapter, since it clearly gives you a new choice for responding to the "shadow" side of your personality. Leaving chapter 5 to experience a little more kindness to and understanding of yourself, you will be ready to begin the path of taking actions that are guaranteed to make you indispensable in the areas of your life most important to you, especially at work.

Making yourself indispensable is dedicating yourself to being "counted on" by others and yourself. Seth Godin makes this point in his book *Linchpin: Are You Indispensable?* when he says, "The only way to get what you're worth is to stand out, to exert emotional labor, to be seen as indispensable, and to produce interactions that organizations and people care deeply about." Just as Oprah Winfrey could be counted on by her audience and Nelson Mandela was accountable to the people of South Africa, you must be counted on by your customers, your manager, your teammates at work, and your family at home. Ultimately, to develop confidence, happiness, and a sense of fulfillment in your life, you must be able to "count on" yourself to honor your commitments that support your growth, your goals, and your play. Thus the core competency necessary to making yourself indispensable is "accountability"— the ability to count on yourself and be counted on by others. Accountability is not determined by an event from your past. Accountability is an ongoing process based on the choices you make each and every moment. Living an accountable life leads to greater happiness, greater learning, and making a meaningful difference to others. Chapters 6 through 11 will walk you through the process of living an accountable life to make yourself indispensable and improve the quality of your life and your success at work. Each of these chapters provides you simple yet powerful exercises to take the information presented and turn it into actions so that you can begin making a difference to improve your life right away. As with any effective road map, not only will you have a clear path for improving your life, but if and when you get off track, you will be able to get yourself back on track with lightning speed using the same road map.

The last chapter provides a summary of the key choices and a road map for making yourself indispensable with some final tips for sustaining success. As many people have discovered, this is a book you will come back to at least once a year as part of revitalizing yourself to achieve new annual goals based on your life's changes.

Making yourself indispensable is sure to increase your level of confidence, sense of security, and ultimate feeling of accomplishment and fulfillment. Are you ready to take the plunge and get started in a process of changing your life once and for all for the better? Let's get started now!

CHAPTER 1:
COMMITTING TO MAKE YOURSELF INDISPENSABLE

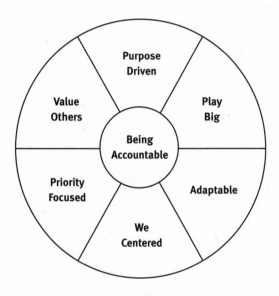

The Wheel of Indispensability

Committing to Make Yourself Indispensable *is one of the most important steps you will take in your life toward being successful and living a fulfilling life. Making yourself indispensable is not about position, power, or ego. It is about taking charge, overcoming obstacles, and achieving your dreams at work, at home, and in your life. Making yourself indispensable is made up of six key spokes listed in the above Wheel of Indispensability, including being Purpose Driven, Playing Big, being Adaptable, being We Centered, being Priority Focused, and Valuing Others. Each* *of these choices will be explored in chapter 1. Ultimately the strength of the Wheel of Indispensability involves being accountable, which is introduced in this chapter and further explored throughout this book. Ultimately, making yourself indispensable is about committing to a bigger purpose than yourself and making a meaningful difference to your organization, your team, your family, and your community. While we all know people who claim to be indispensable, when you have to proclaim it, you are clearly not indispensable. In this chapter you not only will learn what it really means to be indispensable but will have the opportunity to assess your current level of indispensability as a starting point. Finally, you will discovery the essential choices you make each day to either be indispensable or become obsolete.*

"Always bear in mind that your own resolution to
succeed is more important than any other."

—Abraham Lincoln

Making yourself indispensable is for everyone, regardless of your position, role, or lot in life. Thirty years ago people stayed in one organization for their entire career, sometimes as long as forty years. Today many people move to new organizations every two to three years. And even if you aren't changing organizations, how many times have you changed roles and responsibilities within the last six months to a year? Maybe you took responsibility for new technology practices, new relationships with other employees, new processes and procedures, or new skills you needed to apply on the job. Today's business environment doesn't allow for satisfaction with the status quo. It requires constant growth and change. Being indispensable means that you are adaptable, learning and growing with your organization as it changes and evolves. You remain valuable to your organization, to your team, and to the important people in your life. If you aren't changing with your organization, in essence you are becoming obsolete. So at the end of the day, you are either

working to make yourself indispensable or working to make yourself obsolete.

THE TRAP: FAKING YOUR WAY TO
FEELING INDISPENSABLE

Have you ever known someone who "acted" indispensable when
they weren't? Some do this in the form of loud "notice me" or
"bow down to me" behavior or in the form of quietly expecting
others to give them everything without having to work for anything. In either case, these people don't give as much as they take,
which is the ultimate demise of true indispensability. Simply put,
they are annoying at best and destructive at worst. Let's explore the
makeup of those faking their way to feeling indispensable so that
we make sure to avoid this initial trap on the path to being truly
indispensable.

Most of us want to feel indispensable. We want that sense of
security, that sense of control. But some take the shortcut that will
eventually be their demise. There are two general ways of "acting" indispensable when you are still dispensable: power, or force
oriented, and entitlement oriented. Let's explore both in more
detail.

Using power and force to make yourself indispensable is popular with people who have strong egos, financial wealth, or positional power. They make themselves indispensable by keeping
others unsafe, generally through threat. If they have an aggressive
nature, they will yell at others or even use physical force and fear
to make people do what they want. David R. Hawkins, MD, PhD,
describes this well in his book *Power vs. Force: The Hidden Deter-
minants of Human Behavior*: "Power arises from *meaning* . . .
motive . . . and principle. . . . Force must . . . be justified . . . moves
against something . . . [and] . . . automatically creates counter-force."
In a beverage-manufacturing plant in Canada that hired me to
build the management team, one manager would yell at his direct
reports so loudly when they made a mistake that it could be heard
throughout the plant, causing humiliation and embarrassment for

his team. They worked in fear of their manager until they banded together and rebelled. In our personal lives, our spouses and children can feel the same fear when our approach to communication involves emotional or physical mistreatment. The result is hurt feelings, shame, and sometimes abuse.

To act indispensable, some people and organizations use their financial advantage to evoke fear by threatening to take away people's livelihood—whether a job, a home, or the ability to get a loan. Finally, using positional power is one of the most common means of faking indispensability and is most prevalent in the workplace. Employees witness fake indispensability when managers micromanage, dismiss their ideas, or worse, take credit for the solutions implemented by their team.

The second way people create "fake indispensability" is through entitlement. It arises from overprotective parents who never want their children to feel bad about themselves, an education system that doesn't push its students to excel or gives everyone a passing grade regardless of their test score, or a group that encourages people to feel entitled by association (this could be a management level or union). People with an entitled attitude believe they are indispensable based on their mere existence. As long as they are breathing and taking up space at work, they should be paid—even when they aren't producing results. And worse, if they ever start breathing hard (even without satisfactory results), they expect a bonus. In a recent interview, "Tiger Mom" Amy Chua, a professor at Yale Law School and the author of *Battle Hymn of the Tiger Mother*, pointed out different approaches to building self-esteem. We can tell our children that they are wonderful, hoping that they achieve great results. Or we can teach them to achieve great results and use their results as the basis of their self-esteem. Thinking we are the best when we are not is the surest and quickest path to dispensability.

No matter how smart you are, how physically strong you are, what religion, race, or creed you come from, what your financial status is, what abilities and talents you possess, or what positional power you have over others, you are not indispensable unless you use your gifts and principles in service to other people's success, improvement, or survival.

A TRUE PICTURE OF BEING INDISPENSABLE

As a reference point for being and feeling indispensable, let's look at some individuals who are easily recognizable as being indispensable. Of course, these are the extreme examples, but they are the easiest to study for their obvious and public lives that we know so well.

Take a moment and think of the impact of world leaders such as Mahatma Gandhi and Nelson Mandela; country leaders such as Abraham Lincoln and Álvaro Uribe Vélez (president of Columbia); humanitarians such as Reverend Martin Luther King Jr. and Mother Teresa; or public figures such as Magic Johnson and Oprah Winfrey. Some lost their lives by others who wanted them to be dispensable. However, while their bodies are no longer with us, their ideas and influence still last decades or even centuries later. This is true indispensability. What all of the people listed above have in common is that they provided tremendous value to millions of people in all walks of life. They continue to make life better for others through their insights, their inspiration, their leadership, and, most important, through their dedicated actions. They are obvious examples of famous people who made themselves indispensable, not by claiming to be so but through how they lived their lives. More than putting them on a pedestal, it is important that we learn about becoming indispensable by exploring their lives.

While each and every indispensable person just mentioned contributed to massive societal change, they didn't achieve their results without being subject to human frailties. One or more of the people identified above had to overcome each of these imperfections:

- Addictions
- Rejection by others

- Broken commitments and agreements

- Financial loss or coming from poverty

- Physical health challenges

- Imprisonment

- A hostile or violent environment

In other words, no one was handed a positive impact on a silver platter. They had to overcome life's demons, whether abuse by others, their own addictions, or major changes in their lives. They all made mistakes, experienced failure (over and over), and dealt with setbacks. But they never gave up.

BREAKING THE RULE THAT "NO ONE IS INDISPENSABLE"

During my first job while going to university, I heard my boss say to Jimmy, the most competent and experienced employee, who had a very negative attitude that impacted everyone on the team, "No one is indispensable!" Technically, no one is indispensable, since no organization wants to be held hostage by any single individual. So anyone can be replaced. The more important question is "Why do you want to replace this person?" If a person is working hard and providing value, why would you replace him or her? But if the person is like Jimmy—very talented but either not performing or making life difficult for others in the organization— why would you want to keep him or her?

My level of being indispensable bears a direct relationship to others counting on me. People know they can count on me to keep commitments, offer support, communicate fully and openly, and offer solutions that benefit as many people as possible. And when I make a mistake, people can count on me to admit my mistake and offer a way to remedy the situation. People can trust me because they can count on me, and that is what makes me indispensable.

MAKING INDISPENSABILITY REAL FOR YOU

Becoming indispensable doesn't require college degrees, a management role, or a huge income. Anyone can do it. In the next two examples, you will witness how one can become indispensable.

Lynn was one of the six teachers I managed in a specialized school for teenagers. While the students liked Lynn and she had potential to be a great instructor, Lynn was about to be fired—the ultimate sign of being dispensable. She came late and was disruptive in meetings, she allowed her class to get out of control in order to please the students, and the students weren't progressing in their test scores. At her final "corrective action" meeting before being fired, I talked about her future and the choice she had to either waste her talent due to self-serving needs or apply her talent as a value to her students, the other teachers, and the betterment of the school. She had a choice between being liked for the "wrong" reasons and being respected and valued because she made a meaningful, positive difference. Lynn came back to me two days later and said, "I heard your message loud and clear. And you can count on me from now on to be that teacher who is dedicated to my job, my profession, and the school."

Lynn immediately changed her behavior. She came to meetings on time and contributed with great input at each meeting to surface and solve problems. She was more organized in her classroom and spent more time guiding the students in their studies rather than chatting with them just to be friends. She assisted other teachers who were stressed or having difficulty with their lesson plans. Lynn also went back to school to take psychology and business management classes so that she could be more effective in the classroom and prepare herself for a role as a principal. Within six months, Lynn went from being my worst teacher to being my most valued teacher. She became indispensable, and because she had overcome almost being fired, she knew how to teach others on the road to self-destruction to become indispensable. Lynn taught me that regardless of your history, you can make the choice to make yourself indispensable.

Dan was my office assistant for almost ten years. He ran the office and took care of everything. Whether it was a project related to expansion, a difficult communication with a vendor, or a change in office systems, he approached each situation with the highest level of integrity, commitment, and action. He took ownership as if it were his company and assisted me beyond his pay scale and position to lead the organization. He was always looking out for the betterment of the company and for me personally as his manager. We had mutual respect and admiration for each other. Dan taught me that indispensability could happen at any level in the organization. While my moving out of the area ended his employment with me, Dan went on to be a great leader in other organizations.

Based on Dan and Lynn, along with hundreds of other role models I have witnessed during my twenty-five years in business, I have identified ten behaviors necessary for reaching the status of indispensability. For each behavior take a moment and assess yourself by circling one number on the 1-to-10 scale (where 10 is high and 1 is low). Once you have completed your assessment, add up the circled numbers to get your Indispensability Score.

Behavior #1: Be in service to others without expecting anything in return

I seldom take action or communicate with others unless there is a direct benefit to me in the form of reward or payoff.	Low High 1 2 3 4 5 6 7 8 9 10	I regularly take action to support others without any expectation of benefit or payoff for me.

Behavior #2: Be dedicated to the highest standards of performance, teamwork, and communication

I put in an adequate amount of effort in order to "get by" or not lose my job or position.	Low High 1 2 3 4 5 6 7 8 9 10	I am constantly doing my best and achieving higher standards of performance while supporting others and communicating openly and effectively.

Behavior #3: Be open and adaptable

I seldom like change and avoid any new processes, procedures, technologies, or people in my life.	Low High 1 2 3 4 5 6 7 8 9 10	Not only am I open and flexible to change based on new conditions and technology, but I anticipate and respond to change the best I can to be one step ahead.

Behavior #4: Keep commitments and agreements

I regularly make commitments and agreements (to others or myself) but don't keep them due to either legitimate reasons, poor planning, or over commitment.	Low High 1 2 3 4 5 6 7 8 9 10	When I make a commitment or agreement (to myself or others), I keep it, and if a problem surfaces, I let people know ahead of time and renegotiate the commitment for mutual satisfaction.

Behavior #5: Expand your role to support your organization, community, or family

I generally do those assignments or tasks that are clearly my authority, role, and responsibility to do, and I do them within the time allotted.	Low High 1 2 3 4 5 6 7 8 9 10	I take on and perform assignments or tasks outside my "job description" or role in order to support my organization, team, family, or community, and I do this on time or ahead of schedule.

Behavior #6: Be a valued resource to others

People rarely reach out to me except for my special expertise, because I rarely invest the time to be a resource of information, people, or problem solving.	Low High 1 2 3 4 5 6 7 8 9 10	People regularly reach out to me for support, since I am viewed as a valuable resource for information, networking, and problem resolution.

Behavior #7: Be dedicated to self-improvement and professional development

I am good enough as I am and waste as little time as possible learning new skills or improving my performance and communication.	Low High 1 2 3 4 5 6 7 8 9 10	I regularly assess myself and take opportunities to learn new skills and improve my performance, teamwork, communication, and leadership.

Behavior #8: Use obstacles and challenges as opportunities for improvement

When faced with challenges or mistakes I've made, I tend to give up, retreat, or get stuck in frustration.	Low High 1 2 3 4 5 6 7 8 9 10	When facing challenges or mistakes I've made, I persevere to achieve my goals and use those difficulties to learn and improve.

Behavior #9: Engage and include others when making decisions or changes

I make decisions and changes on my own, without input or ideas from others, even though I may think about what is best for them.	Low High 1 2 3 4 5 6 7 8 9 10	I reach out to include others impacted by a decision or a change to include their input and ideas before drawing conclusions.

Behavior #10: Acknowledge and value the contributions of others

I rarely take the time to acknowledge others for their contributions, especially when these are requirements of their role, responsibilities, or commitments and therefore shouldn't need acknowledgement.	Low High 1 2 3 4 5 6 7 8 9 10	I regularly acknowledge the contributions of others based upon their effort or results and let them know they are appreciated for their value.

WHAT'S YOUR CURRENT LEVEL OF INDISPENSABILITY?

If you scored 85 to 100, you are probably feeling fairly safe in your circumstances given normal unpredictable events that can still occur. Even during times of risk, others will want to keep you on the team, because you are such a valued resource in any situation.

If you scored between 65 and 84, you are probably feeling a little vulnerable, but nothing critical. If your situation becomes unstable, you are at risk, since you don't stand out from the pack to receive special treatment.

If you scored between 45 and 64, it is very important to identify areas for improvement and use the process and tools in this book to improve your level of indispensability. You will notice positive results very quickly and begin reaping the benefits of a greater sense of peace, security, and self-confidence.

If you scored 44 or lower, you are in a very vulnerable situation. Because you aren't valued by the organization, you may be given the worst of assignments or be given tasks that you will fail in. But you can change this situation very quickly with a clear intention to do so and by following the process and steps in this book. While it will take some dedication on your part, it is not hard to improve your level of indispensability and get to a point where people want you on their team rather than looking for ways to get you off the team. The choice is yours!

Now that you recognize your current level of indispensability, it's time for you to look at the choices you make each and every day that either contribute to or detract from your indispensability. As you go through the next section, you will discover insights for raising your indispensability to a new level.

MAKING CHOICES TO BE MORE INDISPENSABLE

The choices we make have a direct impact on the results of our life. Our attitudes, behaviors, and actions represent the choices we make. Good news—we can always make new choices if we aren't satisfied with our results. We make an infinite number of choices each day, but there are six fundamental choices that will dictate our life experience. Each choice is presented with a preference for making yourself indispensable, and while clearly these aren't rules but options based on the context of the situation, each preference represents where people tend to have weaknesses that prevent them from becoming indispensable. These six choices have a direct relationship to the degree of confidence and worthiness we feel, the positive impact we have on others, our stress, and the level of safety, fulfillment, and freedom we feel in the world we live in. These are the six choices:

- Purpose Driven or Goal Driven

- Play Big or Play Small

- Adaptable or Rigid

- We Centered or Me Centered

- Priority Focused or Activity Focused

- Value Others or Disregard Others

The six choices above are anchored in the Wheel of Indispensability below. It's the wheel that moves you to higher and higher levels of indispensability. And while these choices, as the spokes of the wheel, are essential to being indispensable, they are demonstrated through being accountable, which means that we are ultimately taking action on our choices.

The Wheel of Indispensability

In different areas of our lives, we may make different choices. For instance, do you play bigger at home than at work? Are you more adaptable at home when your family wants to do something than at work when your teammates want to make a change? As you can see, these choices are not meant to box you into one choice or another. They are meant to identify where you can improve your performance, influence, and communication so that you can become indispensable. As you explore each of these choices, identify opportunities to make different choices to make yourself indispensable or simply to increase your level of self-confidence and fulfillment.

Choice #1: Purpose Driven or Goal Driven (the Master Choice)

I refer to this as the Master Choice because it has the highest correlation to success, indispensability, and personal fulfillment. At work you have goals to achieve customer satisfaction, safety, sales, project target dates, or quality. Effective organizations and individuals establish metrics to measure effectiveness in those areas. And while goals and metrics are essential for achieving success, too often they are established without a clear sense of purpose. As we take action, it becomes about being busy and doing what we are told rather than about making a meaningful difference. For instance, we have all experienced customer service based on a robotic checklist of actions rather than a demonstration of care. Maybe you've had the experience in a restaurant, at the reception desk of your doctor's office, or on the phone with customer service trying to fix your computer or cell phone. The waiter, receptionist, or customer service representative runs through his or her script for "good" customer service—or NOT good! It's an empty experience devoid of the care, consideration, and empathy that make up true customer service. And as if this weren't bad enough, the person ends the conversation with the trite comment "Here at ABC Company, we are dedicated to serving our customers." At which point you get a customer service assessment e-mail, as if you have nothing better to do than take more time to fill out another form.

Goals without a purpose driving them can be destructive, as Daniel H. Pink writes in his book *Drive*. He quotes a group of scholars: "Substantial evidence demonstrates that in addition to motivating constructive effort, goal setting can induce unethical behavior." Bernie Madoff, the infamous financial investor, deemed his goal of making money more important than the people he was serving. He created a Ponzi scheme that caused hundreds of people to lose their life savings.

Goals without a purpose behind them will generally create an "empty" feeling of going through the motions. Customer service is the obvious example you have experienced. But this can also be seen in organizations with safety goals but no sense of purpose behind those goals. A large manufacturing plant I worked with was very focused on safety as a goal but not as a purpose. In fact, there were signs around the plant claiming, "Safety is priority #1." The managers had everyone go through a series of safety training programs in which employees learned safety procedures. The organization had metrics demonstrating its safety record that were measured and reviewed monthly. But even with all of that focus and effort, the organization still had a poor safety record. It was focused on the goal of achieving a good safety record but didn't have a clear purpose for having a safe environment. How do you tell the difference?

While there was a focus on following safety procedures, employees were regularly pressured and reprimanded for not working fast enough. Many times, therefore, employees chose to skip safety-oriented steps in order to meet deadlines. To save money, the organization failed to replace old equipment that was breaking down. This too resulted in safety hazards. And finally, a culture of fear and blame permeated the plant. If someone wasn't wearing safety gear or following a safety procedure, his or her teammate wouldn't say anything because the organization didn't have a safe environment from a communications standpoint.

More important than your goals is the purpose behind your goals. Stephen R. Covey, author of *The 8th Habit: From Effectiveness to Greatness*, says, "When consciousness governs vision, discipline and passion, leadership endures and changes the world for good. In other words, *moral authority makes formal authority work*." If you have a purpose of customer satisfaction, it won't be the checklist that is most important. It will be your care, concern, and dedication to serving your customer that drives your communication, behavior, and actions. You will go out of your way to serve your customer, because that is your purpose.

When you are purpose driven, you are dedicated. In that dedication you will go beyond satisfactory performance or acceptable communication to achieve excellent results.

There are recent examples of businesses that were initially purpose driven, rather than oriented to the goal of making a profit. Mark Zuckerberg created Facebook without a goal of making a profit. He simply wanted to create a vehicle to connect people around his college campus instantly through technology. Six years later, Mark's net worth was estimated at $13.5 billion. Arianna Huffington, creator of the *Huffington Post*, wanted to provide news and education through technology to reach millions of people in response to an increasing monopoly of imbalanced reporting by television networks. Again, in the beginning there was no goal of profitability, but five years later she sold the *Huffington Post* for over $350 million.

When you are indispensable, not only are you purpose driven, but your purpose is "service" to others. I will never forget Rick, a plumber who came to my house to fix a broken bathroom pipe. He was one of the most joyful and cheerful people I have ever met. He loved his job and loved being of service. When he finished fixing the broken pipe, he took a look at the other faucets in the house to make sure that everything was in working order, even though he wasn't paid to do so. He left after fixing a slow drain in another bathroom and replacing a washer in the kitchen faucet at no extra charge. Great service, pleasant experience, and high-quality work because he was living his purpose, not just doing a job. He was the only plumber I ever called back—for ten years now! I wouldn't use anyone else. He was indispensable.

Key Insight #1: Being Purpose Driven Leads to Fulfillment

Goals to achieve personal gain tend to feed the addiction of always wanting more and never feeling satisfied with what you have. Ultimately, it isn't a big leap to turn dissatisfaction into greed. When you are purpose driven, fulfillment is less about having more things. It becomes about the meaningfulness of the things you do have. It is less about the cost or image and more about the value—not only to yourself but to the betterment of your workplace, household, community, and world.

Choice #2: Play Big or Play Small

Some people say that life is a game. If so, you have to determine what game you are in and how you want to play that game. The challenge is that none of us was given the rules of the game when we were born. So we were told what game we were in and how to play it by our parents, our teachers, our friends, and any other influencers along the way. Regardless of which influencers had the biggest impact on us growing up, they were limited by their experience, the game they were told to play, and their own personal limitations. While the guidance we received led to important lessons, at some point we have to make a choice to define our own game and the way we want to play.

Take Mary, for example. She was a supervisor at work and did a satisfactory job supervising her team, but she was continually passed up when it came to promotions into middle management. Mary was actually a very good thinker and had great ideas for improving organizational performance and efficiency, but she had made the choice to "play small." She would compare herself to others and notice that others were smarter and more assertive than she was. She would doubt and second-guess herself, thinking, "What if I say something stupid or what I suggest doesn't make sense?" She sat back saying nothing in meetings or with her boss. Deep inside, she knew she could offer greater value, but she didn't have the courage to speak up. Even encouragement from others didn't help. Playing small impacted her not only at work but also at home. She was the accommodator with her husband and children, trying to please everyone and not taking a stand for what was important to her. Her desire for a loving and intimate partnership with open communication was only an unfulfilled dream.

Only after years of frustration at being passed over at work did she finally ask her boss what she needed to do differently. Her boss was insightful enough to see Mary's gifts as a good critical thinker who could solve problems and as someone with a great ability to coach others. She told Mary about the choice between "playing small" and "playing big." At first Mary recoiled in fear—it was scary to think of exposing herself that way in groups and with her boss—but she realized she was at a crossroads. Either she would have to accept being passed over at work, being subservient at home, and never fulfilling her dreams, or she would have to do things differently and take the risk for a much better life.

After a weekend of soul-searching and assessing her natural capabilities, she decided it was time to share her gifts. While it was going to take courage, the payoff would be the joy and fulfillment she would get from making a meaningful difference and sharing her talents. Being purpose driven, combined with playing big, helped Mary overcome her fears. As a result, she spoke at meetings, adding her ideas even when she wasn't sure how they would be received. She set clearer expectations with her direct reports and did more coaching to improve their individual and team performance. She volunteered to lead projects and drove them to success. She now took charge at work.

Within one year, Mary was promoted into middle management, and she received two lateral promotions within the next three years. At home she went through an adjustment period as she voiced her needs more clearly and represented herself in an honoring way to her husband and children. Although rough going for a while, it eventually led to her experiencing the kind of partnership with her husband that she had always wanted.

PRETENDING TO PLAY BIG

Some people pretend to play big when they are actually playing small. They spend lots of money to impress others, but they do it with borrowed money that puts them in debt. They name-drop people who are truly playing big as a way to impress others.

Truly playing big is about using your talents and gifts in service to a cause greater than yourself. One of the members of my team has a natural capability for managing projects and addressing technology challenges. Even though it is not in his job description, he regularly volunteers to help others in these areas, because he recognizes his gifts, wants to share them, and finds that others value him for it. He is dedicated to playing big and has gained the confidence and accolades that go with it. His generosity has led to his being indispensable.

Unfortunately, some people think playing big is about making demands of others, shouting when they don't get their way, or making others feel small so they can feel big. They are actually playing small with a mask of external behaviors that cause fear and doubt in others. This leads to distrust, the constant stress of holding up the facade, and eventual breakdown.

Once you make the choice to play big by honoring and generously sharing your talents and gifts, you will experience a greater level of self-confidence, a greater sense of contribution and fulfillment, and a greater sense of recognition by others. Playing big is linked to your purpose, and having made those choices, you are ready to make your next choice as you become more indispensable.

Choice #3: Adaptable or Rigid

Robert Anthony wrote one of my favorite quotes regarding anyone wanting to make themselves indispensable: "If you find a good solution and become attached to it, the solution may become your next problem." Rigidity can come in many forms, including your mindset or beliefs, your behaviors, your communication, or your attitude.

Rigidity can come from past conditioning by parents, teachers, managers, or friends, or can be cemented by your own judgments. Rigidity also comes from solutions, procedures, or guidelines that once worked and that you assume will work forever. The good news about rigidity is that it gives you a sense of control—it is predictable. You understand it, know it, can explain it, and can even teach it to others. The bad news is that the sense of control is often a false one or temporary at best.

No matter how hard we try to resist change and remain in control, we are doomed to fail. The world is evolving. We face more technology, increasing customer expectations, greater competition, economic upheaval, and increasing government regulation. Not only is it impossible for us to control these factors, but one or more of these impacts everyone's job at any given time. So the solutions, procedures, and tools we used last year to be high performing may be outdated this year.

The quickest way to become dispensable and lose your job is to remain attached to your old way of doing things, regardless of how you justify it. I worked with a team of software engineers at a major IT manufacturer in the Silicon Valley in California. They were some of the brightest in the business but had a mind-set that they knew what was best for their customers. Within one year, the entire team of software engineers was let go—their jobs outsourced—due to their arrogance, lack of flexibility, and poor customer service.

You can always tell when someone is not adaptable to change. They demonstrate their paralysis through resistance, advocating for the old way, talking about the "good ol' days," or undermining current change efforts through their lack of cooperation and cynicism. Even managers who are supposed to lead change can make the choice to resist it. They show their approval during management meetings but undermine the change when they go back to their direct reports, through either their negative communication or their resistant actions. And worse is when supervisors don't take action on the recommendations of their direct reports to improve quality, efficiency, and/or safety.

Changing times require you to continually question your processes, procedures, mind-set, and attitudes. The only constant in times of change might be your purpose and principles; everything else needs to evolve based on the changing world around you. When you are indispensable, you are continually reviewing the effectiveness and efficiency of your practices, your procedures, your assumptions, and your beliefs. You test everything relative to the changing world around you, and eventually you anticipate the needs of the future so you can begin your response even before the need arises. As you practice this competency of being flexible and responsive, your value and indispensability will increase for any organization dealing with change—namely, any company.

Choice #4: We Centered or Me Centered

While it is each person's responsibility to take care of himself or herself, there is a choice to be made between caring for yourself at the expense of others and caring for yourself in support of others. Unless you are a hermit (if you are, you probably don't know about this book), you are connected to others around you. At work you are connected to your teammates, your boss, other departments that support you in doing what you do, and the customers who purchase or use your services or products. At home you are connected to other family members, extended family, neighbors, and the community you live in. There is very little that you do that doesn't have an impact on the people around you.

Even in the most extreme example, where your job doesn't directly require any input from or connection to others (this is a hard role to imagine), the mere fact that you are doing your unique job means that someone else doesn't have to do it in your place. And when you have a challenge that is isolated to your performance, do you think that you aren't impacting others in your team or organization? We are connected and interdependent with others—in our location and sometimes thousands of miles away.

How many people in the United States were impacted when Japan was hit with one of its largest earthquakes in history, causing a tsunami of record proportions? How many people around the world were impacted when the United States experienced the collapse of its financial industry, housing market, and auto industry? Was it really only a U.S. problem? I think not!

When you have a win, is it really your win by yourself, or were many people part of the win that you get to celebrate? Have you ever had a manager or parent who took all the credit for a team effort or for what you did to achieve success? Not only does it not feel good, but it can cause resentment, disloyalty, and mistrust. Take a moment and do a quick review of your life and the people you've known that had a "me" focus. How did they affect you? Did they ever make a promise to you and not keep it, resulting in a major breakdown or crisis? Did they fail to show up when you were expecting them? Did they ever take an action for personal gain that negatively impacted you and others? Did you have difficulties communicating with them, gaining their cooperation, or getting included when a decision was made, even though you were directly impacted? When people are me centered, they generally aren't thinking about the impact of their communication or behaviors on others. Ultimately, people who are me centered erode trust, teamwork, and collaboration while making it much more difficult to address challenges and difficulties. In the book *The Speed of Trust*, Stephen M. R. Covey writes, "Trust grows when our motives are straightforward and based on mutual benefit—in other words, when we genuinely care not only for ourselves, but also for the people we interact with, lead, or serve." At the core of people's "me" thinking is narcissism and creation of separation between themselves and others in an attempt to maintain control, feel secure, or minimize comparisons when they are feeling unworthy.

One of the common disguises of me-centered behavior is the "us versus them" mentality. While the "us" implies a group, it's still a form of separation that is the core of "me" thinking. It is not inclusive but exclusive.

The greater the "we," the more indispensable you become. At first, being we centered impacts your team. You take actions not only because it is your job to do so but because you are thinking of the effect on your teammates. Once you are dependable as a team member, you are ready to extend your level of influence and expand your level of indispensability, making sure you make decisions and solve problems not only for the good of your team but also thinking of your impact on other departments or functional areas in your organization. This requires greater consideration and understanding or the willingness to ask questions and involve others in your decision-making or problem-solving process. While it appears that you might be giving up control by not making the decision by yourself, you are in fact increasing your level of influence and control of the impact on a larger number of people. This is an essential level of being we centered for anyone in middle or upper management who makes their focus "the good of the organization and its stakeholders," even though it's rarely seen due to silo posturing.

This concept of "we" was demonstrated in Japan in response to the earthquake and tsunami that hit in 2011. Amid the major destruction and resulting shortage of food and water and long lines of people waiting for days to get help, Japanese prime minister Naoto Kan addressed the nation, calling for *ittai*, which means to become "one body." The idea is that as "one body" we all have to take care of one another. Store owners gave away food and clothing without being compensated in order to help others. There were acts of kindness, generosity, and peace, unlike in the similar tragedies in Haiti and New Orleans, where there were anger and looting.

Choice #5: Priority Focused or Activity Focused

When I first entered the work environment as a naive but very eager employee, my goal was to be so organized that I would always complete my tasks and stay ahead of my responsibilities.

I quickly found that even with my best intentions, I fell behind. At first I worked ten-hour days to get ahead, then twelve-hour days, and then weekends on top of that. After one grueling week of ninety hours, I determined that I was in a never-ending cycle and losing battle in which my responsibilities would outlast my effort as long as the organization kept its doors open.

In recent years, many organizations have found themselves with fewer resources while still needing to improve customer satisfaction, develop new technology, and expand market share just to compete in their industry. This requires more resources, but at the same time customers are demanding products and services at lower prices. This means that we have to leverage our time, our efforts, and our resources in order to optimize our results. For example, a government agency outside Washington, D.C., had twenty-three priorities that it needed to accomplish. All twenty-three were being prioritized equally because all twenty-three needed to be accomplished. However, at the end of the year, not one of the twenty-three priorities was achieved. This was blamed on poor teamwork, lack of project-management skills, and lack of resources. The following year the same organization was guided in a process of prioritization where the management team identified two primary priorities and eight secondary priorities. This did not mean that they stopped working on the other thirteen priorities. However, they managed them in such a way as to make sure that the ten top priorities were effectively resourced and took priority over the remaining thirteen. At the end of six months, the two top priorities were completed and six of the eight remaining top priorities were also successfully completed. However, the biggest surprise came when they discovered that ten of the remaining thirteen priorities had also been completed successfully. By focusing on ten, they achieved eighteen priorities, whereas when they focused on twenty-three they achieved none. This is the purpose of prioritizing.

Unfortunately, most people are caught in the cycle of "more is better" and, as a result, keep adding priorities to their already full set of activities. They operate under the illusion that calling something a priority and spending time on it will necessarily make it so. Actually, fragmenting your efforts only keeps you from completing anything. You are like a juggler who keeps adding balls in the air—at some point they all fall to the ground. In fact, unclear priorities are linked to crisis management.

When you scatter your energy, effort, and resources across too many priorities, you risk breakdown from the lack of focus and attention. Mistakes from badly executed handoffs, poor communication, and ineffective decision-making result in crisis. While the tendency is to fix the problem, it becomes a Band-Aid repair. Regardless of the number of fixes you make, you will never outrun the source of the breakdowns itself—the lack of focus and attention.

A secondary challenge to prioritizing is that we have a tendency to value working hard over getting results. We busy ourselves with activities such as unnecessary meetings, e-mails, and bureaucratic procedures to protect our jobs. We ensure that project plans are perfect before starting, making sure that we get buy-in from everyone involved up front but not checking to see if we have enough resources to support the "perfect plan" based on all of the other competing projects being worked on. When we are challenged for not getting results, too often the response is "But we worked really hard; there just weren't enough resources or time."

When other people are fragmented and overwhelmed by the number of projects and tasks they need to complete, the indispensable person assists in creating a sense of calm and confidence through his or her ability to prioritize and set a clear direction that everyone impacted can rally behind and support.

Choice #6: Value Others or Disregard Others

Many people want to prove their value to others and, in so doing neglect to acknowledge others for their contributions. They make sure to put the spotlight on themselves as the "hero" or the "leader" of success. When others offer ideas, these are ignored or dismissed, only to turn up later reframed by the same person who rejected them originally. When a success is achieved, such people will take the credit and ignore the efforts of the many others that directly or indirectly contributed to the good results. While they are trying to make themselves look better, most often it only makes others think they are insecure, needing to boost their ego or make up for an underlying lack of confidence. Truly confident people have nothing to prove in terms of their value and therefore can share the value of success with others. They are more dedicated to developing others and increasing the confidence of their teammates or direct reports than they are to self-promotion. They are builders and givers, while those who lack confidence are takers—taking the credit for what others did or needing others to tell them how wonderful they are.

Valuing others is really about expressing gratitude—letting others know that you appreciate their efforts, their results, and their contributions to successes. Some argue that there is no reason to express thanks, since people are paid to do their jobs. However, think of the number of people who don't get their jobs done or don't pass along needed information. Generally that costs you time, frustration, and even failure. So when someone is just doing their job, you can be grateful that they did in fact get their job done, so that you didn't have to do it for them.

Indispensable people are always looking for ways to help others grow around them. They demonstrate that they value others not only by acknowledging others' contributions but also by helping them to develop and gain new levels of capability and maturity. Others want to be on the team of the indispensable person, because they know that they will grow in the process, which will enable them to be more indispensable themselves. Dispensable people are threatened by the growth of others, worried that others will outshine them, while indispensable people know that their success will only increase through the improved capability of their team.

While these six choices are essential for becoming indispensable, you might be thinking about your life and how out of control you feel to make good choices in your circumstances. You may think, "I had to give up on 'my purpose' at work because of my boss," or "To 'play big' on my team is a recipe for criticism." In fact, you may feel too victimized to think you have an option to become more indispensable. But that couldn't be further from the truth. You just need a new set of eyes for observing an age-old problem.

THE LINK BETWEEN VICTIMIZATION AND DISPENSABILITY

Having control is an illusion. From the moment you were born, you didn't have control of your parents, your location, or the environment in which you were raised, and today you don't have control over economic changes, extreme weather, or even your health. Whatever your situation, you didn't come into this world with a menu from which to choose your ideal life.

As you have grown older, you have probably continued to experience being out of control. Maybe it was a boss who didn't respect you, understand you, or utilize your abilities. Or worse, maybe you were secure in your job and had a history of success and admiration by your boss and teammates, only to be suddenly "right-sized" out of work when the economy shifted or your company was merged with another company. Once again you didn't have control of your destiny. And if your definition of being victimized is being out of control and subject to circumstances that aren't desirable, you can definitely call yourself a victim in this world. Of course, based on that definition of victimization, everyone is a victim. Once you make feeling out of control or victimization an excuse for not improving, not communicating, or not changing your life for the better, you have made yourself dispensable.

You may look at someone else's life and think that their circumstances are better than yours. But you don't know everything about what they are dealing with, such as inner demons, past abuse, or some other form of tragedy. And let's assume they did have it better than you; so what? Let's just assume that your life is rougher, harder, or less desirable than the lives of the people around you; now what? What are you going to do? Give up or go on?

Victimization is a disease that plagues us at home as well, with attitudes such as "You don't understand me," "It's not my job to help you around the house," "It's the teacher's fault that I am failing math or English." Victimization is the death of intimacy and a good, healthy relationship. The relationship becomes about finding evidence that the other person is wrong, unfair, and unreasonable. Whether at work or at home, we refer to this as the "blame game," and when that's your game, everyone loses.

BEING ACCOUNTABLE—THE MOST CRITICAL FACTOR IN BECOMING INDISPENSABLE

We are constantly victims of external changes that we don't control, whether the hurricane in New Orleans that wiped out a good part of that city or simpler changes in our organizations, such as restructuring, mergers, new technology, or a newly hired boss. The question of victimization is not about having control over all circumstances but about addressing how you are going to respond to undesirable events. And once you do what is necessary to remove yourself from harm's way, are you going to use the situation as a roadblock or a stepping-stone to your future? This is the choice that determines if you are living life as a victim or taking accountability for your success—doing the best you can regardless of the circumstances you find yourself in.

Take my friend John, for example. He had been in his job for over ten years. While he was a good performer, it was clear that he wasn't living his purpose, and it was beginning to show up in his results. He was part of a technical team, and he had aspirations of being more creative and starting his own business. But John was afraid to make the move because he needed the income to support his family. After months of his complaining about his

Trap: When You Project Your Past onto Your Future, You Are a Victim

When you are driving a car, do you keep your focus on the windshield in front, with a glance to the rearview mirror, or do you focus on the rearview mirror and glance at the windshield in front of you? Obviously, if you keep your focus on the rearview mirror, you will crash, and the same is true in life. While it is important to learn and adjust based on the past, you want to maintain your focus on the future—taking accountability for creating your own success.

job and sharing his frustration, the company went through a downsizing effort and he was let go from his position. John went into a massive depression and couldn't believe he had been let go, given his ten years of dedicated service to his company. A colleague met with him for lunch and reminded him that just a month earlier he had been complaining that his job was unfulfilling and wishing he could start his own business. His colleague pointed out that this was his chance; with nothing to lose, he could begin his new business and put his entire focus on making it successful without any regrets about leaving a secure job to make it happen. With gratitude to his colleague, he left lunch feeling a renewed sense of purpose, energy, and promise—he was taking accountability for his future rather than being a victim of his past.

THE BENEFITS OF ACCOUNTABILITY

"At the heart of being accountable is the matter of caring," Max DePree wrote in *Leadership Is an Art*. DePree, then chairman and CEO of Herman Miller, Inc., said accountability was "the right of all working people." It's the way to fulfillment, professional and personal.

Success and accountability go together. Happiness and accountability go together. Freedom and accountability go together. Through personal accountability you gain self-confidence, increase respect from others, and expand your influence. Personal accountability is the core value and competency necessary for making yourself indispensable.

When you are accountable, you can be counted on to keep your commitments. You can be counted on to communicate openly, honestly, and clearly, which builds trust and reduces unnecessary conflict. You can be counted on to surface problems rather than hide them, but to also offer solutions rather than complaints. You can be counted on as a support for others. You can be counted on to ask for assistance when you need it rather than waiting until there is a crisis to ask for help. You can be counted on to engage others to solve problems and make decisions, while getting engaged when asked to help out. You can be counted on to learn from mistakes so you don't repeat them. You can be counted on to achieve your goals, which is what leads you to success. And you can be counted on to give credit to and acknowledge those who contributed to success. When you are accountable, you make life better for yourself and others, making you indispensable.

SUPPORT YOURSELF AND ALLOW ME TO SUPPORT YOU

For just a moment, put all of your "yes, buts" aside, along with any other worries, concerns, challenges, and other negative thoughts that you have had before. Trust yourself and trust the process and complete the activities at the end of this chapter to begin the process of changing your life and making yourself indispensable.

Like any journey where you can run into bad weather, traffic, or unforeseen obstacles, the path to becoming indispensable has its challenges. That's why I plan to support you along the way. Yes, my team and I are here for you in case you get stuck or have questions. This is accomplished through our Web site, www.MarkSamuel .com, where you can find several options for gaining support, including

- A question-and-answer section
- Articles and podcasts about being accountable and indispensable

- Accountability Support Communities where you can
  e-mail your questions and provide solutions to support
  others

- Guidebooks and workshops to support you in becoming indispensable

If making yourself indispensable is important to you, then it is important to me, since by definition you will be a major contributor to a more positive world.

The activities at the end of each chapter are designed to assist you in taking action. Whether the ideas in this book are new to you makes little difference. The difference comes from taking action on what you already know and what you just learned and gaining from the ultimate teacher in your life: your own experience. Any idea can be debated forever, but taking action on it is the test to find out whether it works for you.

I am excited you are taking this journey, even if you are starting off skeptical. I respect that and am confident that as you take action the results that follow will over time shape your opinion. Now take a break to complete the activities at the end of this chapter and read on to gain a new perspective around being accountable on the road to making yourself indispensable.

Key Insight #2: Success Comes from Micromovements

Success is not based on how big a step you take. In fact, taking a bigger step than what you can handle can cause you harm, just as lifting weights too heavy for you on your first day exercising can cause injury. The activities in this book are not meant to cost you much time, effort, or work. They are to be viewed as fun, experimental, awareness building, and simple. So keep it easy and simple and remember that perfection is not required. Also, remember that your answers may change over time given what you learn as you continue reading the book.

Exercise—Making Positive Choices

During this chapter you read about six key choices to make yourself indispensable. You will now have an opportunity to identify ideas for improvement by answering the following questions. Don't worry about making a commitment to change or taking action yet. Question 8 below will help you to decide which actions to take first.

1. How would you describe your highest-level purpose? What is the positive difference you want to make in your world that you aren't making effectively right now? Maybe it is being of greater value and support to your team. Maybe it is providing better customer service through a greater level of caring. Maybe it is leading your organization to a new level of excellence or developing others to be leaders. What is your purpose?

2. What ways or in what situations do you tend to play a "smaller" game than your capability, and what is one thing you could do differently to play a "bigger" game to better utilize your natural talents for the benefit of others?

3. In what ways do others perceive you as rigid, and what action could you take that would demonstrate more openness and adaptability to change?

4. In what ways are you sometimes self-centered, and what action can you take to be more inclusive of others on your team or in your family?

5. Where do you tend to get bogged down in lots of activity but achieve little movement toward your desired goals

(Continued)

and results? What action could you take to either prioritize your top three to five projects or goals or eliminate needless activities?

6. What action can you take to acknowledge others at work or at home and let them know that you appreciate their input and effort that is contributing to overall success?

7. What action can you take to stop blaming others for a problem and put that energy into developing alternative solutions you could eventually share with others?

8. Based on your answers above, which one to three actions would you commit to taking within the next few days? Your criteria for choosing your one to three actions should be based on likelihood of success.

9. Track your results as you take action and notice the impact inside of you in the form of self-confidence, clarity, or sense of peace, and notice the impact on others in the form of positive influence, cooperation, and trust.

Now that you have made a commitment and new choices for becoming indispensable, you are ready for your journey. As with any journey, it is best to have a clear road map to get you to your destination. The foundation of becoming indispensable lies in taking personal accountability on the job, at home, and in your life. This road map gives you a clear, step-by-step process for avoiding the Victim Loop and stepping onto the Accountability Loop moving up the trail to indispensability. As a result of implementing this road map, you will experience greater self-confidence, *influence, and fulfillment, not to mention greater success at work and ultimate indispensability.*

> "We are what we repeatedly do. Excellence, then, is not an act, but a habit."
>
> —Aristotle

M aking yourself indispensable is the destination, and personal accountability is the road map. It is the pathway to becoming an effective leader in your life regardless of your position—to take command of difficult situations, adapt to change, and take advantage of new opportunities. It is a neverending process. After you reach one level of success, you will have a path to an even higher level of success. Executives, supervisors, individual contributors, and people managing their families and homes have used this road map to achieve their goals, expand their positive influence, and manifest their dream life at work and at home.

THE MYTHS ABOUT ACCOUNTABILITY

For a moment please forget everything you have been told about accountability—even by other experts. Forget blaming and finger-pointing. Forget "who is responsible for this mistake?" Forget the definitions you've heard, the conversations you've had, and the negative connotations about accountability that you might be holding on to. "Accountability is heartless." "Accountability is too hard." "Accountability only serves business." "Accountability is about metrics." "Accountability is about people looking over your shoulder and pointing out your failings." Erase everything and start over with a clean slate.

Accountability is not just keeping all of your commitments. Accountability is not just doing what you say you are going to do. While those are popular and simplistic viewpoints, they aren't a complete picture. For instance, what if you have a commitment to attend a meeting at work, and on the way to the meeting room, you pass a person who is sitting down, bent over, obviously in some kind of discomfort or pain. No one else is around except you and the hurt individual. If you stop to ask if the person needs help, you will be late to your meeting, thus not keeping your commitment—not honoring your agreement to show up to the meeting on time. What would the accountable action be in this case? Of course it is to stop and assist the person, even if it makes you late to the meeting you committed to attend. So what is true accountability?

PERSONAL ACCOUNTABILITY AS A LIFE VALUE AND COMPETENCY FOR SUCCESS

Whether your desired outcomes are ones related to the workplace, such as high customer satisfaction, impeccable quality, supportive teamwork, inspiring leadership, growing profitability, or the highest level of safety, you must take the actions necessary to achieve those results. At home, if you want to experience a loving family, in which your children are prepared for higher education or a great job when they finish school or in which you share intimate communication in a positive and supportive relationship with other family members, you must take actions and demonstrate behaviors that are consistent with those desired outcomes. You could have a desired outcome of making more money and be so lucky as to win the lottery, but if you aren't taking the actions necessary to sustain your wealth, you will spend your fortune until it no longer exists. In the example above, while it was a desired outcome to attend the meeting on time, there was a bigger desired outcome to be of assistance to another person in need when no one else was around to help.

Accountability Defined

Accountability is taking action that's consistent with your desired outcomes.

Knowing your desired outcomes is the key to accountability. If you don't know where you are going, it is impossible to get there. In other words, if you aren't clear on your "picture of success," it's almost impossible to be successful.

- For Michael Jordan, his "picture of success" meant going from not making the basketball team in high school to becoming the best player to ever play the game.

- For Steve Jobs, his "picture of success" meant believing he could bring Apple back from the dead to become a leader in its industry.

- For Oprah Winfrey, her "picture of success" meant rising from a childhood of poverty and abuse to become one of the most powerful and influential women in television.

- For Mahatma Gandhi, his "picture of success" meant pursuing India's independence from the British Empire. Gandhi "lived, thought and acted, inspired by the vision of humanity evolving towards a world of peace and harmony," said Martin Luther King Jr. Gandhi clearly knew where he was going.

Whether your goal is to become indispensable at work, at home, in your community, or in your country, beyond having a clear picture of success you must also take the actions necessary to accomplish that picture of success. But it all begins with defining your picture of success.

THE PERSONAL ACCOUNTABILITY MODEL— YOUR ROAD MAP TO SUCCESS

When you drive across the country, it is critical that you have a road map. The map tells you the path to take in order to reach your destination successfully. You get to choose whether you go there slowly or more quickly. However, if you take a shortcut, you

risk getting lost or losing your way. However, the value of a good map is that even if you get lost or sidetracked, you can use the map to find out where you are and make the adjustments necessary to get back on track.

The Personal Accountability Model was developed in 1985 and published in 1986 as the first accountability map of its kind. Created in response to a team that was stuck and unable to perform due to a massive dose of "blame game" victimization, the model not only worked to get this team unstuck but has been used by thousands of people to achieve success in their workplaces and create a higher quality of life at home.

The model starts when a situation comes up—and it's usually a challenging one. Based on your *intention*, you have a *choice* as to how to respond. When you take the victim road, you *ignore* the problem, *deny* your involvement in it, and eventually *blame* someone else. Then you *rationalize* and justify why another person should take care of it and *resist* any attempt that others may make to get you involved. Finally, you *hide* to avoid dealing with it.

Given the same situation, based on an intention to *stay accountable*, you make a different choice. You *recognize* the problem and take *ownership* of getting it resolved. You *forgive* yourself and others who may have contributed to the problem. You are then in a position to *self-examine* how you contributed to the problem and *learn* what you can do differently to resolve it. Finally, you *take action* to implement your new solutions so that you can deal with the challenge and learn from your experience. This model is the basis for the remaining chapters in this book. You will learn each step of the model and how to apply it to your goals and desires. As in the first chapter, you will have an opportunity to do exercises at the end of each chapter to bring the concepts and tools to life. Through your clear picture of success, your actions, and your learning along the way, you will achieve a greater level of indispensability.

RESIST RESISTANCE

With so many benefits to being accountable, why do so many people resist it? It was when I reviewed the areas of my life in which I was stuck, not achieving my goals and desires, and not being seen as indispensable to others, that I discovered my own reasons for not being accountable. In the next chapter you will have the opportunity to explore your resistance to accountability and identify barriers that you put up that prevent your success. The remaining chapters will be your road map for turning those stumbling blocks into stepping-stones to success. There are three fears that keep people from being accountable and indispensable:

- Fear of Blame
    - We associate accountability with blame. We fear that if we're accountable for something, we'll be the one to get blamed if it goes wrong. Blame triggers feelings of shame and inadequacy, and nobody wants to feel those. When we avoid being accountable, we might not get blamed for making mistakes, but we end up getting blamed for not accomplishing anything.

- Fear of Failure

  - None of us wants to look bad, make mistakes, or feel incompetent. To avoid feeling that way, we play it small. We stay in what is familiar. We don't challenge ourselves with bigger choices, so we don't have to ever feel inadequate. If we don't take risks, this is as good as it gets. The fear of failure prevents us from taking risks that might produce mistakes. But mistakes are one of the best ways to learn, and learning is the only way to improve. Fear of failure guarantees falling short of success.

- Fear of Success

  - If we are always setting goals of being more successful and lying awake at night thinking of ways to be more successful, how can we be afraid of success? Because while we want to be successful, there is a part of us that knows if we are more successful, then we will take on more responsibilities and need to meet higher standards. And maybe we won't be able to handle this new level of responsibility or expectation. Deep down, we don't want that extra pressure to perform, so we sabotage our success. Sometimes we aren't afraid of more responsibility, but we are afraid of people's jealousy and our own guilty feelings for outperforming others. That is a lot of pressure, and who wants to deal with that? It is much easier to dream of success than to actually achieve it.

CLEARING THE PATH AHEAD

Putting all fears or concerns aside for a moment, you are ready to take the leap onto your path of accountability on your way to making yourself indispensable. However, before you plant new

Exercise: Preparing Yourself for Success

Achieving success isn't a process determined by perfect scenarios or circumstances. We all have our challenges. Some are internal thoughts and concerns, while others are external factors that present us with obstacles. The key to success is using your strengths to minimize or move through your challenges. This exercise will help you to surface both your challenges and your strengths as a jumping-off place to begin your accountability process and become indispensable.

1. What items at work could you be more accountable for in order to raise the level of respect that people have for you or to reduce the stress caused by not being more accountable?

2. What are the rewards for increasing accountability at work? at home?

3. What are your fears or concerns about being more accountable?

4. What can you do to support yourself in reducing your fear or gaining assistance from others?

seeds for growth, it is important to clear away any undesirable weeds or rocks that are in your way. The next chapter aims to give you the ability and skill to identify those weeds and rocks that have been stumbling blocks in your past, so that you can begin to address them effectively, freeing you to be fully accountable for creating your desired outcomes and picture of success. As in any garden, weeds and even rocks can show up again as the seasons evolve, so it is important that you keep an eye out for those victim responses that show up inside you and sometimes get expressed. Remember, these are normal human behaviors, and the key is taking command over your historical reactions and learning new approaches for steering yourself back to your goals and pictures of success when those reactions occur.

After taking a little time completing the exercise to take action on this chapter, turn to the next to start eliminating those beliefs, attitudes, and behaviors that have prevented your success until now.

CHAPTER 3:
THE VICTIM LOOP

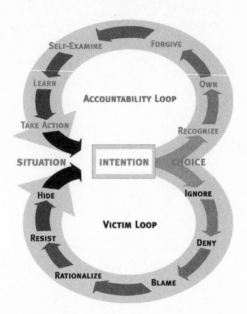

The Victim Loop *is a way of life in which "stuff" happens to you. You don't seem to have a choice. Since we all visit it at different times in our lives, the question to ask yourself is not "How do I prevent myself from going there?" but "How fast can I get out of there?" If you choose the Victim Loop when faced with a challenging situation, you ignore, deny, blame, rationalize, resist, and ultimately hide from it. As much as you don't like living there, take a look at what happens when you go to the Victim Loop.*

"No snowflake in an avalanche ever feels responsible."

—Voltaire

I t is a common experience to find yourself in difficult or even
terrible circumstances. The worst of these are when you come
into harm's way—contracting a disease, being physically threatened, being forced to file bankruptcy, or getting evicted from your
home. However, it doesn't require a major incident like these to
cause you extreme upset or disturbance. Daily situations like getting cut off while driving your car, getting a new project when you
are already burned out, or failing another test in school can result
in high levels of anxiety, fear, anger, frustration, or hurt. Regardless of the situation, the question remains the same: *What are you
going to do now?* These events aren't what make you a victim.
What makes you a victim is how you respond to these events. When
you respond with *accountability*, you may feel the pain of the
situation, but you move forward anyway and achieve your goals
in spite of your difficult circumstances. You do the very best you
can, learn from your mistakes, and go on to achieve success. But
when you respond *as a victim*, you begin a downward spiral that
moves you further and further away from your goals—making
you more dispensable as you continue on the victim path.

FEELING STUCK—THE PLIGHT OF VICTIMIZATION

How do you know when you are in victim mode? The surest sign
is that you feel stuck—stuck in feeling angry, hurt, frustrated, or
discouraged; stuck in your job; stuck in your relationship at home;
or stuck in physical pain. You are spinning your wheels without
coming up with new solutions to an old problem. Ultimately, when
you have been stuck long enough, you wonder, "Why me?" Everyone seems against you and you can't seem to get a break. You are
suffering and you don't know what to do about it. Following are
three examples of people who found themselves in victimization

that we will come back to throughout our journey: an employee, an entrepreneur, and a senior manager. Yes, victimization is experienced regardless of intelligence, position of power, age, or previous success, as you will see in the examples below.

Paula—an Employee with Promise

Paula was an intelligent and highly skilled employee with a successful past. She was hired as an office manager at my consulting firm. My friend Jeff had recommended her, and on paper she seemed to be a perfect fit for the position. Like anyone new on the job, she made mistakes. Oddly, she always had an excuse. She blamed the computers, the employees who worked for her, even clients, and she never apologized or corrected her errors. Everything that went wrong was always someone else's or something else's fault. And it was always beyond her control. The morale on her team was plunging, and her leadership qualities were being questioned. She was behaving as a victim, almost as if she had nothing to do with what was going on.

She rarely took responsibility and never learned from her mistakes. She was regularly coached on ways to improve her organizational skills, communication, and basic leadership skills. Despite our efforts to assist Paula in becoming more accountable, improving her performance, or developing her leadership skills, results never changed and it was never her fault. After several months we parted ways.

When you don't acknowledge the impact of your attitude and behavior on your current dilemma, you lose the power to do anything about it. And when you blame others, the equipment, not having enough resources, or anything outside yourself for the problems you are facing, you are in victimization mode. Leadership is not a position but a role that you can play in any position at work or at home. And if you desire to be an effective leader at work or in your personal life, victimization won't get you there. It's impossible to lead your team to higher performance, better teamwork, increased efficiency, or improved morale if you are blaming others when problems surface. While leaders are solving problems, victims complain about problems or use them as excuses to explain failure.

Deborah—a Struggling Entrepreneur

Deborah was a successful employee and manager working for a large organization. Based on her success and desire to be more independent, she left her job to go into business for herself as a consultant. To get herself started, she formed collaborations with several other consultants. Unfortunately, while collaborating with other consultants gave her the promise of income until she could build her own business, it kept her from focusing on her core competency of assisting others in her core area of strength involving marketing plans and strategies. Her business was very up and down, always showing promise but never becoming the fulfilling venture she had dreamed of. She worked harder and harder, but with no return. After a while, her confidence eroded and she began to blame herself for not being smart enough, competent enough, or effective enough to build her business. She even tried to return to a job within a corporation, but she never got hired. When the economy shifted downward in 2008, she found herself devastated, with no clients, no income, no promise of getting hired, and a feeling of hopelessness.

Even with hard work and lots of effort, you can be stuck in victimization. And if feeling stuck leads to blaming yourself, you will be in one of the deadliest victim stances.

Chris—a Successful Plant Manager

Chris was a very successful manager who was hired in his twenties on the shop floor and soon became a supervisor and manager, ultimately rising to the position of plant manager. Chris got results. He had high expectations and was very directive and very decisive. He worked long hours and demanded obedience from each member of his management team. When a problem surfaced, everyone knew to bring it to Chris for a solution. He was smart, quick, and great at determining root causes to resolve organizational problems. After several years of successful growth, the organization faced a new and formidable challenge. Increased competition, customer demands, and technological advancements required Chris's plant to drastically increase its effectiveness while implementing major technological changes at a time when resources were being severely cut. His managers weren't keeping up with the changes and were coming to him with problems more often than ever. While Chris was spending longer days at work and working weekends, his plant was failing to get the improved results necessary to meet corporate goals. It didn't take long for Chris to begin blaming his direct reports for failing. No amount of threats or even daily tracking of results was producing successful results. For the first time Chris was failing and being threatened with the loss of his job.

His need to be in control and to have the answers, which had served him well in the past, was now his Achilles' heel. Yes, even when you appear accountable and seem to be taking charge, you can still be operating from victimization.

Each of these people provides us a great opportunity to explore what takes us into victimization, since the first step out of being stuck is awareness. They also provide the inspiration for and keys to getting out of victimization and taking accountability for achieving our goals and becoming successful. While all of the individuals presented here demonstrated being stuck in victimization, they also eventually found their way back to accountability and demonstrated that the game of life is never over until we make it so. You'll see the evolution of these people as they become more accountable and more indispensable in chapters 5 through 12. No matter what our failings or how stuck we may be, there is a way out, and you will learn that way out as you read on.

CHOOSING VICTIMIZATION

"Victim" is a paradoxical word. Most people think they are victims when they don't have a choice. In fact it is the opposite: We

Victim Loop

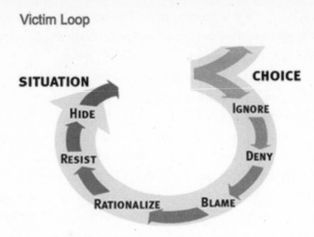

are actually *choosing* to be victims even when we don't realize that is the choice we are making. "Victim? By choice? No way. Not me." That's the response I usually get when I discuss this with clients.

In this next section, you'll read about the infamous Victim Loop, and you'll see how you are often the one who sabotages yourself and keeps you from achieving your goals.

Where and how does the Victim Loop start? It always starts at the same place: You are faced with a challenging situation, and you make the choice to look the other way. That's all it takes.

TYPICAL RESPONSES TO A TOUGH SITUATION: THE SIX PHASES OF THE VICTIM LOOP

None of us are immune to visiting the Victim Loop. Falling into the victim mode doesn't make you a horrible person or inadequate in some way. There's no need to punish yourself; you are simply being human. It's just a bad choice on the menu of life. But what can you do about it? You can either eat the meal in front of you, despite the fact that it doesn't taste very good, or you can order something else.

The sooner you realize you are in the Victim Loop, the sooner you can recover and get back to the business of achieving your goals. But how can you recognize when you are about to enter the Victim Loop? How can you catch yourself in advance so you don't make the same victim choice over and over again?

There are six common phases of victimization that make up the Victim Loop. They don't always come in this order, but there is an underlying logic to how they progress. That's why we call it the Victim Loop. As you become more aware of each phase of victimization, you can take dominion over it. Will learning the six phases of victimization cause you to never become a victim again? No. It will happen, even for those of us who teach this model. But knowing the model and applying the methods and tools taught when we review the Accountability Loop will assist you in lessening the time and suffering you spend in victimization.

Phase #1: Ignore It: "Problem? What Problem?"

Sound familiar? This entry into victim mode is a classic. It's called ignoring the situation, and at some time or another we all do it. At the office you may avoid addressing a breakdown, resist starting a tough project, or ignore conflicts with your coworkers just to get through the day. At home you may put off dealing with your aging parents or perhaps fail to schedule a needed doctor's appointment because you don't want to find out about a potential health issue.

One of the first questions to ask yourself is *why* you are ignoring a problem. You may be ignoring it deliberately, because there is something else more important to deal with at the moment. In this case, you are making a responsible choice. We live in hectic, complicated times, and not every problem can be solved the moment it appears on our radar screen. We prioritize, and that's a good thing.

But if what you're really doing is pretending the problem doesn't exist . . . and hoping all the while that it will disappear by itself or that someone else will take care of it for you . . . you've just entered the Victim Loop. And the problem with ignoring problems is that they usually get bigger—problems turn into crises, crises turn into breakdowns, breakdowns turn into lost jobs and eventually going out of business. When problems are ignored in organizations, they become underlying diseases that, when surfaced, elicit the response "That's just the way we do things around here."

In the example above, Paula, the employee with promise, ignored the feedback she received from management that her leadership wasn't working. To protect herself from having to address her own attitude and behavior, she became blind to the severity of the problems that were stemming from her poor performance and communication.

Phase #2: Deny It: "It's Not My Problem"

Sometimes problems get so big that you can't ignore them any longer. Instead of acknowledging and learning from a small but repetitive mistake with a long-term customer who forgives you based on your relationship, you make the same mistake with a new customer, who decides to cancel his or her order due to higher expectations. If you still don't want to deal with the problem, you can continue on the Victim Loop by denying your responsibility for the situation. Not sure what it sounds like when you get there? Here are examples to help you identify it:

"Other customers don't think it's a problem."

"Sure, there's a problem, but it's not *my* problem."

"Hey, it's not my job."

"Nobody told me."

"My last manager didn't make me do this."

The reason some people deny they've had anything to do with the problem is that the pressure is building and they're not willing to take responsibility for it. From that perspective denial can make sense, but that doesn't mean it works. You are now part of the problem.

Denial is a tricky place to be, because if the problem isn't yours to solve, that means it is someone else's responsibility, which leads you to further entrench yourself in victimization. For the organization, problems don't get resolved unless someone is assigned responsibility.

Phase #3: Blame Someone: "It's Their Fault"

Attention, all victims. This is the moment you've been waiting for—the chance to point fingers at other people, the chance to play the blame game. That's right, the blaming is about to begin, because if I'm not responsible, someone else surely is. And better them than me.

The rules of finger-pointing are pretty easy to follow: Surface a problem, find someone else to blame, and blame away. At work you can do it with your managers, other departments, associates, or "the corporate office." At home kids can blame their parents, parents can blame their kids, and of course, spouses can blame each other. If you're unhappy with your financial state, you can blame the economy, spiraling unemployment, or budget deficits. There is always someone or something to blame. And you can even feel a false sense of control, domination, and power by blaming others. Thus, blaming is popular with children and adults alike. Just observe children on a playground or listen to politicians on an election campaign.

Deborah, the struggling entrepreneur, and Chris, the plant manager, both demonstrated blame-game posturing, but in very different ways. Deborah blamed herself for the problems, criticizing her poor decision making, her lack of business savvy, her ineffectiveness, and a never-ending list of other judgments. While some view self-blame as taking ownership, there is one major difference. Taking ownership is focused on solving the situation, while self-blame is focused on beating yourself up for the past, which you can no longer do anything about.

Chris blamed his direct reports for not following his orders or implementing changes to improve effectiveness and achieve the metrics that were part of the weekly and daily dashboard process. No amount of yelling or reprimanding his team was getting different results.

Even when people are labeled complainers or whiners, they still find it hard to call it quits. But be careful: The blame game is a double-edged sword, and you will probably get blamed in return. In fact, in fear of being blamed, people are already prepared with an idea of who they are going to blame to get the finger pointed elsewhere instead of at them. Organizations can create a culture of blame and "CYA" as the means for solving challenges. This can go on with no end in sight and only leads us deeper into the Victim Loop.

Phase #4: Rationalize It: "I Have Evidence"

It's hard to maintain the blame game without proof that we are right. Thus, it is time to rationalize and justify our position. So we look for evidence that we don't need to do anything about the problem. Evidence that someone else is responsible for it. Evidence that we are right and someone else is wrong. At this stage, meetings get scheduled, surveys are taken, and we call friends to feed our side of the story. We do anything to justify our lack of ownership. We convince others that our boss's decision was wrong, that we don't have enough resources, or that it's not our fault that our performance isn't better. At home we find evidence that our spouse isn't a good communicator or that our children aren't grateful enough. One way to rationalize is to make comparisons with others who appear to be in similar positions. Look how smart they are, how many resources they have, how their product has better features than our product. You can always make a comparison to another's situation and come out on the bottom. Poor you!

Rationalization is the favorite playing field of the mentally gifted—those who have strong analytical skills. The smarter you are, the easier it is to get trapped in this stage—even using spreadsheets, graphs, surveys, and benchmarking to make your point.

Paula used rationalization to justify her failure, claiming that she didn't have sufficient resources or good enough equipment to be successful. She compared our consulting firm to the last organization she had worked in. Chris used the data presented in his dashboard reviews to blame his people for not performing. Instead of using data to engage others in problem solving, he only focused on proving to people that they weren't getting the job done. And Deborah used the results of other more successful people in her field to prove that she was incompetent.

Whether evidence and data are used to blame others or yourself, you're working a lot harder to avoid the situation than you would need to work to deal with it. And because you are working so hard, you are setting yourself up for the next level of victimization: *resistance*.

Phase #5: Resist It: "You're Not My Boss!"

When all else fails . . . get angry—throw a tantrum. Why not? It's normal to resist injustice and tap into the two-year-old inside of us who's struggling to gain control.

Control is the issue and power is the goal. You know you're in it when you hear yourself deliver self-righteous pronouncements like:

"It's the principle of the thing."

"I don't work for you."

"You can't make me."

This is the point in the Victim Loop when conflict and irrational action start escalating. You are far from the original situation, and you are still not dealing with it. In marriages, this is when a debate about who'll take out the garbage turns into a full-on relationship-threatening battle. In work situations, this is when an argument over who is selected to be on a special task force causes people to start damaging their careers.

When Paula was still working for me, she refused to take feedback or implement the new systems being implemented for improving operational excellence. Paula was fully entrenched in victimization with no way out, and everyone knew it. There is only one way left to avoid embarrassment, and that is the final phase of victimization: *hiding!*

Phase #6: Hide from It: "You Can't Find Me"

This is the last stage of the Victim Loop. Having exhausted all other methods of avoiding the situation, you go into hiding. It's amazing how some people truly hide. You simply can't find them anywhere—they're not at meetings, their voice mail is full, and they don't respond to e-mails. They've actually disappeared. And boy, are there lots of good ways to hide. Here are a few.

Create busywork. Go ahead, overwhelm yourself with meaningless activities. Then you are too busy to respond to important priorities or breakdowns that are more challenging to address. Create unnecessary meetings, paperwork, and projects. At home, do laundry again, vacuum the carpet, open mail, do *anything* that looks important to avoid dealing with the real issue.

Generate a crisis. Feed the rumor mill, share information that doesn't really exist, withhold information that someone needs, tattle on your sibling, do anything to create a diversion from the real problem at hand.

But the best way to hide? Stay confused! This is especially effective during times of change—new processes, new technology, or a new structure at work. You can even pretend to support a change when you have no intention of implementing it. You can say, "I think this change is a great idea, but because I don't understand it well enough, I will need to keep doing things my old way until you can explain it to me better—but don't see me as negative, since I support it a hundred percent."

Before the economy completely wiped out Deborah's consulting business, she would spend much of her day organizing herself "to become more effective." She would run from one networking event to another, mingling with other entrepreneurs struggling as she was, even though those meetings didn't produce new prospects or leads.

Chris spent his time doing more and more micromanagement. In fact, it got so bad that he would have meetings with people two and three levels down the organization to manage their tasks by going through checklists. He looked like he was being account-able when in fact he was stifling his organization by his overcon-trolling posture.

Successfully going into hiding means you've effectively com-pleted the Victim Loop. A dubious achievement. But if you want to make a good case for why you are failing, why you are being let go from your job, your marriage, your dreams, I am sure you can blame someone and prove it! Of course, you are only proving your dispensability. You are not needed by anyone except other vic-tims. And there is no greater validation than to become part of a group of victims, all discussing how life isn't fair and the world is an unjust place to live. But when the pity party is over, you are stuck with yourself in the self-doubt created by knowing that you aren't achieving your goals or your picture of success.

VICTIMHOOD IS A DOWNWARD SPIRAL

Here's the strangest part of victimization. It takes more effort to play the victim and justify why you can't solve a problem than to be accountable and do what it takes to resolve that same problem. It's a lot of work to create new ways to blame people, resist being accountable, and find good hiding places. Yet it is a competency that people are developing at all levels in many organizations today.

The ultimate irony is that if you had been accountable to begin with, you would have successfully dealt with the challenge long ago. Not only that, but instead of being the villain you would have been the hero.

When a weight lifter stops lifting, the muscles atrophy, and so it is with accountability and the ability to address challenging sit-uations. The longer you avoid dealing with those difficult situa-tions, the harder it is to respond to them when they confront you.

In the long run, it's actually *easier* to be accountable.

One of my consulting assignments involved teaching Account-able Performance Coaching at a high-tech company. Two years after taking this class, Tom, a first-level manager, called me for advice. Sue, one of his employees, was spreading rumors about his poor leadership. I asked him what he had done already to resolve the situation. He responded, "At first I didn't do anything, hoping that Sue would stop fabricating these negative stories. When the rumors continued, I asked Sue to stop, but nothing changed. I trusted that the team members were mature enough not to believe her stories." "Then what happened?" I asked. He responded a little more sheepishly, "The whole team turned against me."

I asked Tom if he had gone to his human resources adviser. He responded, "No. I didn't want anyone to think I was a bad manager and couldn't handle my team. Besides, this isn't my doing. Sue should be the one blamed for this problem." Finally I asked Tom how bad the situation was. He said, "I went to lunch, and when I came back the entire team was gone!" When Tom looked for them, they were all sitting in the HR adviser's office sharing their disapproval of Tom.

My advice to Tom was simple. Document the rumors and the escalation of the problem. Then meet with your HR adviser to discuss solutions to the problem. After our talk, I asked Tom if he was clear on what to do next. He paused. I could tell something was wrong. Again he said, "If I go to the HR adviser for assistance, they will think I am an ineffective manager." I pointed out the obvious: "Tom, you no longer need to worry about being perceived as an ineffective manager. You are ineffective!"

Tom was stuck in the victim cycle, ignoring the problem, blaming Sue, resisting support, and hiding from those who could best support him. Tom was caught in one or more of the toxic beliefs or emotions commonly experienced by those in the Victim Loop.

THE TOXIC BELIEFS OF THE VICTIM LOOP

Beliefs can drive behavior and emotional reactions. There are certain beliefs or mind-sets that promote victim responses, which is where self-sabotage begins. Some of the most toxic beliefs include "I'm right," "It's unfair," "I can't," and "It's not my style." Let's explore them further.

"I'm Right!"

We love being right and we hate being wrong. This goes to the very core of being human and wanting to feel validated, valued, and respected or even admired by others. Sometimes we will do anything to be right, even if doing so has a negative ramification for ourselves. Have you ever seen two people arguing when they are making the same point in violent agreement, just to prove that their way of saying it is right and the other person's is wrong? Unfortunately, having to be right to feel a sense of self-worth results in ignoring problems that stem from you or your area of control. This causes you to blame others, resulting in rationalization and hiding to prevent having to admit that you were wrong or made a mistake.

"It's Unfair"

People want life to be fair. We all understand that. We want to have equal opportunities, we want equal say in decisions that impact us, and ultimately we want life to go the way we have it planned. But this is an illusion stemming from our need to control. Life isn't fair, doesn't provide equal opportunities for everyone, and rarely goes the way we have it planned in our heads. Whether it's a natural disaster, a decision by your boss, or an unconscious act by your child in a moment when he is truly "acting his age," it comes upon you as a disruption if not a crisis—which catches you by surprise and appears unfair. Having the mind-set of "It's unfair" leaves you in the Victim Loop of denial, blame, and rationalizing.

"I Can't"

This is one of the most powerful beliefs. Henry Ford said, "Whether you think you can or you think you can't, you are right." When you say, "I can't," you immediately cut off any possibility of coming up with alternative solutions to address a difficult situation. When others are asking for help, you are busy rationalizing why you don't have the ability, intelligence, or time to deal with the situation. It is a certain way to become dispensable, since it will be preferable to find someone who thinks they *can* deal with a problem rather than someone who thinks they can't.

"It's Not My Style"

"It's not my style" is one of the most relied upon excuses and has unfortunately been reinforced by the development of style surveys and assessments. When your way isn't working and someone offers an alternative, instead of trying out a new way of doing things in hope of a better result, the victim approach is to denounce the new way as not fitting into your style. I recently came across a sales team that wasn't producing results. A newly hired manager requested that the team do things differently, at which point the team objected because the new manager had a different style. No one thought it might be a good idea to follow the new manager's direction, given that they weren't achieving acceptable results. Using the "It's not my style" argument is a sure way to prove that you are more dedicated to being comfortably mediocre than to becoming uncomfortable enough to get successful results.

THE TOXIC EMOTIONS OF THE VICTIM LOOP

Behaviors produce emotions. When you act as a victim, your behaviors create emotions that have the power to poison your personal and interpersonal relationships and undermine your success. The most toxic of these emotions that I've identified are guilt, resentment, disappointment, and mistrust. Let's explore them further.

Guilt

Even if you won't admit it out loud, you feel bad about yourself when people can't count on you. It lowers the self-esteem and confidence necessary for accomplishing your desired results. You feel guilty about avoiding responsibilities and betraying someone's trust in you. Guilt is a judgment you have *against yourself.*

Resentment

When you resist accountability, anger is a way to push away the people holding you accountable. You attack others to protect yourself and justify your position. The bitterness spills over into your relationships and negatively colors your perceptions. Resentment is a judgment you have *against others*.

Disappointment

Disappointment begins with an expectation of how something will turn out. When our plans aren't actualized in the way we wanted, we are set up for a disappointment. The problem with disappointment is that it easily leads into discouragement, hopelessness, and depression. It is based on the need for control and the fact that we aren't in control, especially of anything involving others. Disappointment can result in our drawing conclusions that we aren't good enough, that we aren't worthy enough, or that others are against us. Disappointment is a judgment *that you, others, or life have let you down.*

Mistrust

When you consistently refuse to deal with situations, people stop trusting you. They might not always realize it consciously, but they just know they can't count on you. In their eyes you are always part of the problem and never part of the solution. Mistrust is a judgment *others have against you.*

SO NOW WHAT?

Now you can start to work toward achieving your dreams and goals. When you move from being a victim to being accountable, you regain power over a life that might feel like it is passing you by. Falling *in* the Victim Loop is never the issue. The issue is how fast and efficiently you are getting *out* of it. On your way to becoming indispensable, you will meet challenges and obstacles. The question is how to overcome them when they show up. Are you willing to change some of the habits that have gotten you in

Exercise: Getting Past Victimization

In preparation for turning your life around or moving to your next level of excellence, complete the following two assignments:

1. Make a list of all the situations and relationships in your life that you want to be better. These might include getting back in charge on your projects; dealing with an uncooperative coworker; improving your communication skills; or changing your career.

    Be specific. Write down at least five areas for improvement. Place an asterisk by those items that are the most important to you. Refer to this list as you receive additional guidance in exercises in the following chapters.

2. Make a list of the most common patterns of victimization that you use that have undermined your success or contributed to the situations that you want to improve. Without any sense of blame, review these as an objective investigator. Without making any kind of commitment to never do those behaviors again, which won't work, just take notice when they show up in the future. As soon as they become less automatic and more of an observable choice, you will be able to make a new choice, and gradually they will become less powerful in your life.

the situations that you want to change? So how do you get out of this Victim Loop?

In the following chapters, you will learn practical strategies and tools for living a life of accountability. Following the order of the Accountability Loop, which I refer to as the A-Loop, each chapter will provide an in-depth study of a step in the process of being accountable, including the ways to avoid slipping into the

Victim Loop. Through following the steps of the A-Loop, you become an A-Player in your own life and a person who is indispensable. Don't forget to do the exercises at the end of each chapter to begin putting these strategies and tools to immediate use. You will find a way out of the exhausting cycle of victimization and into a new level of accountability and indispensability as you implement these strategies and tools.

Take a breath. It only gets better from here.

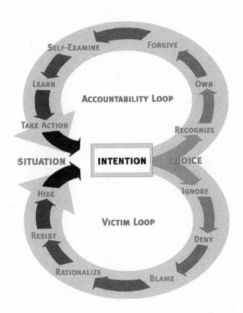

Intention to Take Charge of Your Life *is no small task. Although it is a simple path paved with common sense, it certainly is not an easy one to travel. Make it important; stick with it, because life is no rehearsal. This is it. Life is happening right now. Make sure you choose wisely to become indispensable to those you value, whether it be on your job, in your family, or in your community. And by all means do it for yourself, so you can experience the best life possible. Creating a clear intention is part of developing that Picture of Success that represents your destination and changes your focus from victimization to accountability. Intention not only is used to get out of victimization, but it is the first*

step to becoming purpose driven (a concept discussed in the first chapter) and increasing your indispensability.

> "If you want to build a ship, don't drum up people to collect wood, and don't assign them tasks and work, but rather teach them to long for the endless immensity of the sea."
>
> —Antoine de Saint-Exupéry,
> author of *The Little Prince*

Most people don't realize they have choices. They think they are victims of their circumstances, their background. They think that, because they were born in this family or with these handicaps or in that country, they can or cannot do something. There are any number of examples where these truths have been challenged; people rise up from poverty, people without legs run marathons, and the visually impaired read and write books. Those who have overcome their difficult circumstances had a picture in their mind of a better future. Based on that picture, they learned what was needed and worked hard to manifest their picture as their new current reality.

Often what is missing for people who are stuck in a negative circumstance is a picture of a better future. They are picturing only the negativity of their past or their current situation. You have to be able to see or envision or perceive yourself as a pianist before you can become one. If you can't picture what success looks like, it is very hard, if not impossible, to achieve that success. Can you imagine painting a horse without a picture of it in your mind ahead of time? Can you imagine building a successful business without having an idea of what the business will offer in terms of product or service? Can you imagine what it is like when you just show up to work, but with no clear picture of what successful performance looks like? You are lost—just going through the motions of doing what you are told to do and falling short of expectations.

In this chapter you will have the opportunity to create a picture of your success. A clear description. In your career it may be finding a fulfilling job, becoming the top performer on your team to set yourself up for a promotion with expanded responsibilities, or a role in leadership. In your personal life it may be meeting your ideal mate, determining the best college to support your education, building your dream house, or writing the book you always dreamed of sharing with the world. Whatever your thing is . . . what does it look like and feel like? Clarifying your intention and Picture of Success is the basis for every other step along the A-Loop (Accountability Loop). In fact, without a clear intention and Picture of Success it is very hard to be accountable.

PERFECTIONISM: THE FAST TRACK TO PARALYSIS

Accountability begins with discovering what you want. What difference do you want to make for yourself and for others?

To be able to answer this question, you need to clear the deck. Start fresh, so you are free to create without limiting your imagination. There is one pattern that is often confused with accountability, and it is most paralyzing: *perfectionism*. And it is a dangerous trap. It seduces us, because we think it equals accountability and is required for success. Quite the opposite is true— perfectionism actually *prevents* success. Many people's definition of accountability is to do what you say you are going to do or to keep your commitments. When our humanness shows up, mistakes happen and our perfection is broken, and then we blame ourselves or get blamed for not being accountable enough. But perfectionism fosters inaction—waiting until we can guarantee success before we take action. And this negates accountability and prevents success. We wait for the perfect plan, the perfect decision, and the perfect action that won't possibly fail. "Perfectionism is the enemy of creation," John Updike said. It *stops* you from taking risks, looking for new perspectives, and solving problems with original thinking. In fear of seeming awkward or being blamed for a mistake, people don't explore creative ways. Although excellence is a *process* of continual improvement, perfection is *a final state* against which you judge yourself.

There are many examples of our most successful and innovative leaders demonstrating imperfection on their way to becoming legends. One such legend was on intimate terms with failure. He failed in business twice and suffered a nervous breakdown. He regularly lost elections, including one run at his state legislature, three congressional bids, two Senate elections, and one bid for the vice presidency. After all those failures, he became our sixteenth president. Abraham Lincoln led the United States through the most crucial period in its history. He won the battle to keep the country united, and he ended the horrific institution of slavery. Lincoln accomplished all of this in spite of his far-from-perfect record of prior losses.

TAKE RISKS WITHOUT GAMBLING

Part of leading a successful life is taking risks, and you can't wait to be perfect to start taking them. If you think you have to be perfect before you can be successful, you quickly trap yourself in the Victim Loop because you have made yourself a victim of your lack of perfection. From there your slide further into the victim mode happens fairly easily as you let your lack of perfection become your excuse for not taking action. Some people are worried about taking risks because of the possible costs if something goes wrong.

Even people with great talent had to make mistakes on the path of becoming indispensable.

Don't believe me? Just look at the Beatles. They were one of the most famous and successful bands of all time, and some people believe they had a near-perfect career. In reality, they are a great example of four people who didn't quit when they had setbacks along the way.

Legend has it that the Fab Four took America by storm and were overnight sensations. This couldn't be further from the truth. The three singles they first released in the United States had little or no impact. In early 1963, Chicago-based Vee-Jay Records issued the Beatles' first two U.S. singles: "Please Please Me" and "From Me to You." Neither did very well; the latter made it to number 116 on the Billboard chart before slipping into obscurity. In September of the same year, "She Loves You" met a similar fate. If the Beatles had quit at this point in their career, we never would have heard of them.

It wasn't until December 1963, when Capitol Records launched the largest PR campaign in music history around the single "I Want to Hold Your Hand," that the Beatles began to move into their success. The Beatles' 1964 American tour and an appearance on *The Ed Sullivan Show* sealed it, and Beatlemania was born. What's revealing about this example is that we only remember the Beatles' success, not the missteps and the struggles along the way. If they had stopped their journey on the road to success because they weren't perfect from the get-go, they never would have become the Beatles as we remember them.

The net result of perfection is paralysis. The good news is that being accountable has nothing to do with being perfect.

THE MIND-SET FOR HIGH PERFORMANCE

It is impossible to become indispensable without a mind-set for high performance. Ultimately it's your mind-set that leads to achieving your work goals, fostering positive and trusting relationships, and developing credibility with your customers and upper management. There are three essential elements to raising the bar on your mind-set of excellence: creating a clear intention, defining and refining your Picture of Success, and testing your picture for enough "stretch" to make a meaningful difference. When put in place, these three things will lead you to a compelling destination that will drive every action you end up taking along the A-Loop to achieve your dreams of becoming indispensable.

Step 1: State Your Intentions and Set Your Ultimate Goals

There is no accountability without intention. *Intention* represents the desired purpose, goals, and outcomes that are the basis of your plans and actions. If your intention is to be a top performer and team player, then it wouldn't work to show up late to meetings, be uncooperative with your teammates, or fail to complete your assignments on time. However, without a clear intention, your negative actions and behaviors don't matter to you, because there is no specific target or purpose that you are trying to accomplish. As Lewis Carroll stated so clearly, "If you don't know where you are going, any road will get you there."

If I told you I ate a hamburger, fries, and a milkshake for lunch, nothing would be wrong with that. But if I told you that my intention was to lose weight and lower my cholesterol, then you would know I was off track. Intention represents your ultimate purpose and desired results. If your purpose is to be indispensable, then your intention describes your service and value to others. In the case of Habitat for Humanity, its intention was to make sure every family had a home. For Zagat, it was making sure people had a consistent and accurate guide for choosing restaurants with a high level of predictability. Magic Johnson had an intention to develop retail stores that reflected the needs and desires of African Americans while bringing forward a new standard of excellence to people of less means and opportunity. This is what you do by acting with accountability.

Your intention could be starting your own business or creating a positive team environment at work. It could be improving customer service or ensuring a safe environment at work. It could be developing the most positive, loving, and supportive relationship with your family, or it could be dedicating yourself to your spiritual growth and evolution. Regardless of your intention, you are not dependent on others to make it happen. It is all about you.

When creating your intentions, be true to yourself, your best self containing the wisdom, practicality, and intuition that know what is best for you and others. Your intention represents the combination of your purpose and "playing big" (from our discussion in chapter 1) based on your unique talents, capabilities, and opportunities to make a meaningful difference for others.

When Deborah bottomed out as an entrepreneur during the economic downturn, she did some very intense soul-searching to rediscover her intention. She relooked at what difference she wanted to make and at her unique attributes. Included in this self-discovery was identifying what she loved doing—loved it so much that she would do it without compensation. In an attempt to generate revenue, Deborah had linked herself with other consultants to deliver team-building programs, provide project-management training, and facilitate communications workshops. She realized that through these efforts she had lost her sense of her purpose. Her real love was marketing and helping people to brand themselves in support of building their businesses. She also loved to network people in order to find solutions. She had lost her way in pursuit of financial gain, but now she was reenergized and back from the miserable feeling of defeat and victimization. Having a clear intention is one powerful remedy for feeling stuck, discouraged, hopeless, and even depressed.

You can create intentions around any goals you want to accomplish. Your imagination is what limits your intention. So what's stopping you from achieving anything you want? Maybe you want to be the best car salesman in the dealership or the most respected leader. Maybe you want to be a great parent or design a great Web site or eradicate cancer or save the dolphins. Declaring your intention clearly is the foundation for maintaining a positive focus and breaking free from the Victim Loop.

Let me tell you the story of Jerry, who experienced one of the biggest and fastest transformations based on creating an accountable intention to become indispensable. He was the plant manager for a division of a utility company. His plant was not delivering on expectations, and morale was low. Jerry blamed corporate leadership for its lack of support and his management team for being in the Victim Loop. It isn't uncommon for people in the Victim Loop to see others as victims. I was hired by corporate to coach Jerry.

If Jerry didn't improve plant performance, then corporate leadership would remove him as plant manager. So, the people he blamed for his poor results were going to remove him based on those results—a double bind. The first assignment I gave Jerry was to create his clear intention of leadership. He answered the question "What kind of reputation do you want to have with your direct reports, customers, and upper management—how do you want others to see you?" Jerry articulated in three long paragraphs that he would like to be a trusted leader who got results. He described himself as being decisive, responsive, and open to change. He shared his intention of engaging his management team and employees in solving the problems of the plant. Jerry found his intention to be energizing and inspiring. Now, instead of focusing on how corporate leadership and his management team were letting him down, he was more interested in how he was going to make his intention come alive. Jerry's posture, energy, and connection with others immediately changed for the better as he began to embody the mind-set of his intention. Creating a clear Picture of Success enabled Jerry to get out of the Victim Loop. Based on his Picture of Success, he developed better systems of tracking, led his team in problem-solving efforts, and was more confident in working with corporate leadership to resolve the challenges in his plant. Instead of wanting to fire Jerry, now corporate leadership trusted him to lead his organization to success.

Intention is the first step: It represents your commitment. You still need to figure out what success means for your own challenges and aspirations.

Having an intention puts you on a path of achievement; having a clear intention makes the path easier to follow.

Step 2: Picture What Success Looks Like to You

Once you have a clear intention the picture of success enables your intention to come alive. The picture of success describes the attitudes, behaviors, and actions you would be exhibiting once you are accomplishing your intention. It's difficult to reach a goal if

Exercise: Clarifying Your Intentions Big and Small

Start by dreaming big. What is your purpose? How do you want to be of service to others? What would you be doing even if you weren't paid for it, just because you love doing it? What gifts and capabilities of yours would you like to share with others? Answer these questions to get an idea of your intentions.

you don't know what it looks, sounds, and feels like. The clearer the picture, the easier it is to accomplish.

Four Questions to Develop Your Picture of Success

1. What are you accomplishing?

2. How are you accomplishing it?

3. How does it feel to be accomplishing it?

4. Who else is supporting you while you are accomplishing it?

CREATING YOUR PICTURE OF SUCCESS

As you will see, Paula's Picture of Success includes very descriptive and specific behaviors. She chose behaviors indicating a "stretch" that describes how she will behave, communicate, and take action differently from how she has in the past in order to demonstrate a higher level of excellence. When crafting your Picture of Success, you want to avoid philosophical statements, such as "I believe the customer comes first." This sentence doesn't describe a behavior you are taking. You also want to avoid outcomes or results, such as "Customer satisfaction improves by 10 percent." While you may desire that, unless there is a behavior attached to that statement, it doesn't belong in your Picture of Success.

Paula's (the Employee with Promise) Future Picture of Success

My intention is to be valued as a top performer and contributor to my team and organization. I am recognized as a leader among my peers. My customers, managers, and teammates can count on me to keep my commitments, communicate effectively, and provide support. I am well organized and anticipate challenges or roadblocks to be solved in order to demonstrate my proactive nature. My performance and results consistently meet or exceed others' expectations.

Management and members of my team view me as responsive. I listen well, check for understanding, and follow through to completion. If I am not able to keep a commitment or run into an obstacle I can't handle, I surface it immediately and get help so I can complete my project or task. My positive attitude and behavior contribute to a positive work environment.

I am constantly learning and developing my skills so that I can take on more responsibility and adapt to the changing business environment. I openly pass along my learning to other team members in support of improving performance and communication.

Your Picture of Success should include descriptive behaviors and actions you are taking that demonstrate what you are doing differently to achieve better results, such as "I am giving customers my full attention, openly listening to their needs and goals, and responding in the most effective and timely manner with a positive, pleasant, and professional manner." Finally, even though you are writing descriptors that you aren't yet exhibiting consistently, you gain the most power of this process by writing them in the present tense, as if you are doing them now. Refrain from statements that include "try" or "attempt to." Be bold and claim what you want to be doing without hesitation.

While there are no set rules for creating your Picture of Success, it usually includes the following four sections:

1. Behaviors, attitude, and actions to improve your service to internal or external customers

2. Behaviors, attitudes, and actions to improve your com-
    munication, coordination, and support of team mem-
    bers or people you work with in other departments

3. Behaviors, attitudes, and actions to improve your rep-
    utation with management

4. Behaviors, attitudes, and actions to continue your
    professional and personal self-development

Step 3: Test Your Picture of Success

If your Picture of Success isn't clear, you won't know what to do
to get better results. If your Picture of Success isn't enough of a
"stretch" from your current level of excellence, then you will
waste your time with lots of activity but will not achieve significant improvement. And the challenge of creating a Picture of Success is that it can sound good but not be effective. There are a few
ways to test your Picture of Success. This isn't a pass-or-fail type
of test but a test that guides you in making the necessary changes
to achieve a higher standard of performance, communication, and
teamwork.

Testing your Picture of Success begins with reviewing the six

---

Exercise: Create Your Picture of Success

Based on the guidance and three steps above, create a *clear picture of success*. Be as specific as you can in describing what it
looks, sounds, and feels like to consistently exhibit behaviors,
actions, and attitudes that reflect a higher level of excellence
and lead to greater success. It doesn't have to be perfect. As you
read it and use it, you will refine it. As you continue in this process and test it, you will discover ways to make it better. It is a
work in progress, and the only way to fail is to not do it at all.

choices to being indispensable that we discussed in chapter 1 to ensure that your Picture of Success is comprehensive. While you were instructed to develop your Picture of Success based on the first two choices ("purpose driven" and "play big"), it is important to relook at them when you are testing. You can answer the following questions to assist you in testing your Picture of Success. Remember that the purpose is to look for any ways in which you can make your Picture of Success clearer or more of a stretch.

1. Does your Picture of Success clearly articulate your intention and purpose in such a way that when you wake up each day, you are clear about what you want to accomplish?

2. Does your Picture of Success convey a clear picture of what you would be doing and how you would be communicating in order to "play big" and courageously?

3. Does your Picture of Success include your ability to adapt as conditions change in your work environment, in your personal life, or in general?

4. Does your Picture of Success include impact on and benefit to others, to ensure that you are "we centered"?

5. Does your Picture of Success provide you a clear sense of priorities, so that you can be focused on the essential aspects of your Picture of Success?

6. Does your Picture of Success include how you will demonstrate your value of others, both in terms of their input and in terms of your acknowledgment of their support?

After answering each of those questions in order to fine-tune your Picture of Success, you are ready to determine whether it is a meaningful stretch to improve your level of excellence. This is accomplished by asking yourself on a scale of 1 to 5, where 5 means you

Chris's (the Plant Manager) Future Picture of Leadership Success

My intention is to lead my organization in a turnaround that raises our standards of performance and achieves the challenging goals of our organization. I have a reputation for having a clear picture of organization success. I include the senior management team in developing a sound, practical, and clear strategy along with focused priorities that lead to success. I ensure aligned and regular communication of our priorities and picture of organizational success to the entire organization.

I effectively lead the senior management team and middle managers in developing an accountable culture of high expectations and support, cross-functional and team collaboration, engagement of employees at all levels of the organization, and absolute focus on our priorities. I am known as a facilitator of change rather than a dictator of change. I foster critical thinking within the management team and assist them in solving problems and removing obstacles to higher performance.

I have a great relationship with corporate leadership, and they trust our strategies for improvement, our tracking of commitments and progress, and our results. They view our plant with the highest regard and use us as an example to others for customer service, efficiency, change leadership, and producing results in an environment of high morale. While I am responsive to the needs of the corporation, I effectively negotiate requests to ensure that our plant has the resources to achieve our deliverables and business results.

are already consistently living your Picture of Success and 1 means you have a very long way to go before you are consistently living it, how would you rate yourself currently? In other words, based on how you function consistently today, what number would best indicate your current level of impact based on the criteria in your Picture of Success?

If you scored between 1 and 2.50, then your Picture of Success is excellent because it demonstrates a high level of clarity and stretch. If you scored between 2.51 and 3.50, then you are in a good position to make some improvement, but it would be better to get a little more specific in the areas of your Picture of Success that would provide more clarity about your behaviors, reactions, communication, and actions. If you scored between 3.51 and 5, then you should strongly think about reworking your Picture of Success to make it more of a challenge for you, less philosophical, and more detailed as to what you will be doing differently when you are indispensable.

COMPARING TWO DIFFERENT PICTURES OF SUCCESS

Two men were carrying rocks on the side of the road. One was complaining and hating every minute of it. The other one was whistling and clearly having a good day. A third man came along and asked, "What are you doing?"

The complainer answered: "Can't you tell? I am carrying rocks."

The whistler answered: "I am building a cathedral."

While one man was a victim to his circumstances and had a tiny Picture of Success (getting through the day), the other man had a huge purpose for himself as part of a team building a cathedral. Each man's Picture of Success and view of his role determined his attitude, performance, and communication. In addition, his picture determined his quality of work life—and life in general.

Does your Picture of Success convey carrying rocks or building a cathedral?

Now that you have defined your intention and created a Picture of Success, you have completed one of the most critical steps in being accountable. From now on, as you move forward and run into any obstacles that get you discouraged, frustrated, or disappointed, take out your Picture of Success as a reminder of where you are headed. Remember to keep your eyes on the windshield, not the rearview mirror, as you travel through life. One method for using your intention with a Picture of Success is a concept often used by engineers and project managers called reverse engineering.

REVERSE ENGINEERING

One trap that organizations and individuals fall into when they desire a major change rests in their approach. They define their goal for change as being state B. The current organization is in state A. After analyzing state A and its problems, they move into improvement processes in order to solve the problems existing in the state A organization. This makes perfect sense, except for one thing. They are in the mind-set of their current state, state A, when they are solving the problems surfaced. When they complete the improvement effort, they have only created a better state A, not necessarily a new state, state B. In fact, many of the problems solved didn't need to be solved, because in state B those problems may no longer exist. Albert Einstein described this best: "The significant problems we face cannot be solved at the same level of thinking we were at when we created them."

"Reverse engineering" is the term industrial companies use to describe the process of starting with a final product, state B, and working backward in order to figure out all the elements needed to create it. If an organization wants to gain efficiency and effectiveness by breaking down the silos and improving cross-functional execution, it would picture no silos and effective cross-functional execution and establish new ways of functioning to match this image. This is very different from identifying all the ways in which the organization currently doesn't operate cross-functionally and making improvement. The change happens faster, and the change is made using the new state B way of handling change and making decisions.

For yourself, identify the change you want to make and picture it already changed in the most successful way possible. Then picture state B in as much detail as possible—what it would feel like, what conversations you would be having with others (including who those others would be), how you would be supporting yourself, and how you would be addressing problems that surfaced along the way. Then, from that clear description of state B,

Exercise: Keeping Your Intention and Picture of Success Alive

It's one thing to create your Picture of Success and another thing to keep it alive and have it mature inside of you. This exercise involves determining a regular time for you to review your intention and your Picture of Success. It doesn't have to take long—just three to five minutes at the most will do. Maybe you would like to use it for starting your day on the right foot. You can have it by your bedside to review in the morning as a reminder. Maybe it is better for you to review before going to bed, so that you get to sleep on it during the night. Some people just make it a weekly review, picking one day a week that is best for them to review it, digest it, and make it real inside them.

Warning: The purpose of this review is not evaluation to determine how well you are doing based on your Picture of Success. The purpose is to integrate your Picture of Success into every cell of your body. Ultimately your goal is not to achieve your Picture of Success but to embody it.

Extra Credit: If you want to boost your Picture of Success even further, please send us a copy at our Web site, www.Mark Samuel.com, and look for the link called "Extra Credit." We will give you feedback with suggestions for improving your Picture of Success.

start taking action to implement state B behaviors, communication, and actions. You don't need to ever look back at state A or worry about the problems of state A when your focus is on state B.

> I never hit a shot, even in practice, without having a very sharp, in-focus picture of it in my head.
>
> —Jack Nicklaus

You are ready to move on the road map of the A-Loop. In the next chapter you will recognize your current reality, an important step in determining what has been getting in the way of your being more successful and achieving a greater level of indispensability.

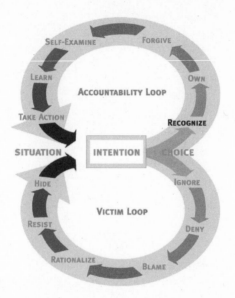

Call it what it is. Whatever it is. Be honest. Until you know what you are dealing with and are willing to call it out, you can't do anything differently. This is the step for beginning to take dominion over those barriers preventing your success and keeping you from being indispensable. Sometimes they look really big. But when you shine the light on them, it turns out they weren't as big as you feared. After you have defined your intention and developed a Picture of Success, recognizing your current reality is the first step in taking accountability to manifest your picture. So pull out your flashlight and take a look.

> "It often happens that I wake up at night and begin
> to think about a serious problem and decide I must
> tell the pope about it. Then I wake up completely
> and remember that I am the pope."
>
> —Pope John XXIII

C lear *intention* and a *Picture of Success* give you direction. In order to take your next steps, it is important to recognize where you currently stand in relation to where you are going. With honesty and courage, you need to determine what is working and what is not working. This step is not an assessment to determine root-cause problems or find solutions—a common mistake for people in a hurry to solve problems. Why not solve the problem as soon as you can? First, because you may be spending time attempting to solve a problem when other more important problems go unsolved, and second, because at the earliest stages of surfacing a problem, it is easier to drop down into the Victim Loop by looking for someone to blame. Recognizing your current reality has two main parts: identifying as many strengths and opportunities for improvement as possible and prioritizing the opportunities for improvement based on your current situation and what will move you forward to achieve your Picture of Success.

A FUTURE-BASED CURRENT REALITY

When *identifying your current reality*, common practice is to compare where you are today with current standards of excellence or with where you have been. While this is important for acknowledging progress, it can lead you astray from your *intention* and off the Accountability Loop. In the previous chapter, you learned about moving from state A, your current state, to state B, your Picture of Success and desired future state. When you identify problems of state A that have little or no relationship to achieving state B, you can solve those problems, but you will only achieve an improved state A. You won't necessarily be any closer to your Picture of

Success. Let's remember that our purpose is to achieve your Picture of Success to fulfill your intention, not just to get better.

I had the good fortune of working with a technology-based organization that was considered the benchmark in its industry worldwide. When its leaders identified their current reality, their average score on all of the criteria important to their Picture of Success was 2 out of a possible score of 5 (5 being high). I immediately asked, "How is it that you are the benchmark in the industry and only scoring two out of five on most of your criteria?" The response was stated clearly: "If we scored ourselves based on current results or our past, we would give ourselves five out of five, and we could pat ourselves on the back as we claim success. However, five years from now, our competition will have caught up and surpassed us. Our picture of success includes being the benchmark in the industry five years from now and our average score of two represents the gap between where we are now and where we want to be. It is not suggesting that our performance is poor in our current state." Your current reality measures the gap between your current performance and your desired future state described by your Picture of Success.

LET'S BE HONEST

If your intention and Picture of Success involve improving your performance and communication, then you must answer questions such as "What aspects of my performance and communication do not match my ideal standard of excellence?" If your intention is to spend more time with your family, the very first question is "How do I spend my time now?" The answers to either question will be areas you can improve or interpret as current weaknesses. But how do you assess your current reality without going into negative self-judgment—feeling bad or getting discouraged?

Ultimately, to achieve your intention you must face your current reality, no matter how "bad" it appears to you. There are two ways to build your inner strength to face your current reality—a neutral frame of mind and a courageous heart.

A NEUTRAL FRAME OF MIND

Very much like the battery in a car—where the positive and negative polarities depend on each other to generate electrical power—a neutral frame of mind has positive and negative elements, but these do not carry a bias of good or bad. They just are. The reason most people have a hard time assessing the reality of a situation in their own lives is that they can't remain objective and unbiased. When they look critically at their own lives, that analysis comes with judgments and resentments, guilt and disappointments. But the work of accountability requires a *neutral* mind.

To become accountable you need to really look at what *is*, not what could have been, should have been, or would have been. With a neutral mind, you don't need to feel threatened by the truth. It is what it is, and there is no need to hide or judge. At this point in your journey, you don't need to find solutions or fix anything. You just need to look at what supports your goals and what doesn't. It is that simple.

It's simple, but it's not necessarily easy. Being neutral requires a dedication and persistence. Our minds will wander into negative thoughts about ourselves or others. Our feelings will get stirred into disappointment, resentment, or guilt.

Therefore, it takes vigilance to call "time out" to this familiar process and bring back a neutral mind. Some people create their own "recovery plan" by taking a walk or calling a friend when they spin down. Be careful not to select a method for getting back on track that is self-destructive, such as overworking, surfing the Net, or reorganizing your desk . . . again. My favorite destructive method used to be food. I would use it when I was challenged by uncomfortable feelings and self-judgment. It worked to calm the critical voices, but only temporarily, and my pants size expanded accordingly, which resulted in additional critical voices.

Jack Welch, the retired legendary CEO of GE and *Fortune* magazine's "Manager of the Century," describes the same mindset when he talks about "GE's decades-old principle of reality." In Robert Slater's book *Get Better or Get Beaten!*, Welch says: "Let me try to describe what we mean by reality. It may sound simple, but getting any organization or group of people to see the world the way it is and not the way they wish it were or hope it will be is not as easy as it sounds. We have to permeate every mind in the company with an attitude, with an atmosphere that allows people—in fact, encourages people—to see things as they are, to deal with the way it is now, not the way they wish it would be."

To ease the journey toward attaining a neutral frame of mind, it is critical to enhance your compassion—for yourself and others. This path is one of understanding. There is no need to blame ourselves or others. If you had *known* how to do any of this better, you would have *done* it better. The mind can fool us into thinking we already know something when in reality our emotions and body don't know better yet. For example, while I knew it wasn't great for me to eat candy when in airports, my emotions didn't know a better way to calm the stress I felt when traveling. Therefore, willpower was only a temporary solution to a deeper issue. It's a healthier approach to trust that the current negative situation is a great setup for learning. Living is not an easy occupation. Let alone attempting to lead a life that is deliberate, fun, loving, and aimed at high performance and standards of excellence. Learning is necessary, but facing our current reality in order to learn from it is often painful.

Compassion is about *caring*. It's about caring more about improving weaknesses or making situations better than about finding fault and pointing fingers.

A COURAGEOUS HEART

High performers and those who are indispensable are constantly in the game of *recognizing their current reality*. They have their antennae up for anything that is getting between them and their Picture of Success. They are dedicated to facing, prioritizing, and systematically doing what it takes to remove those obstacles.

Others ignore their current reality, whether that means accepting mediocre performance at work, allowing communication breakdowns, or not managing their finances to stay out of debt. They are so impacted by their embarrassment, disappointment, discouragement, and poor reputation that they will do anything to avoid a negative self-assessment. However, they become stuck with whatever is keeping them from their Picture of Success and from becoming indispensable.

Being accountable is a path for the courageous. You must have a strong heart and confidence in yourself to face your current reality—to look in the mirror and see the truth without exaggerating your strengths or your weaknesses. It is an honest, bold look at yourself, your team, your organization, and your family. When you are accountable and on your road to becoming indispensable, you have the courage to search for the truth even when it could cause you disturbance. You don't cover up. You don't escape. You don't pretend. You don't censure or play CYA games. You boldly admit what doesn't work and you trust that you have the strength and resources to eventually find solutions.

With a compassionate, neutral mind and a courageous heart you are now prepared to recognize your current reality absent blame or judgment. You are now ready to prioritize your current reality in order to focus your efforts moving forward.

A COMPREHENSIVE REVIEW OF YOUR CURRENT REALITY

Your Picture of Success is the reference point for assessing your current reality. In other words, you aren't assessing your current reality based on current standards of excellence, but on future standards of excellence necessary to support achieving your Picture of Success. The following sections provide a list of criteria to get you started. This is by no means an exhaustive list, but it will provide you a basis for identifying strengths and areas for improvement related to many areas of your life. To make this process simple and relatively quick, rate each criterion on a scale of 1 to 10 where 10 is strong and 1 is weak. Your rating is based on the extent to which your performance today is a positive contributor to your future Picture of Success. Remember that a low score *does not* mean that you are performing poorly in that area based on current standards. It only means that based on your Picture of Success, current performance doesn't measure up to your future desired reality.

Once Paula, the promising employee, developed her Picture of Success, she took the next major step of recognizing her current reality. It was major because she knew before she started that there were many aspects of her performance and communication that weren't working. In fact, she was very nervous about feeling discouraged and worthless after completing the assessment. She called a friend for moral support, took a deep breath, and reminded herself that the assessment was a necessary step to achieving her

Personal Excellence (Based on Your Future Picture of Success)

Customer Complaints	Low High 1 2 3 4 5 6 7 8 9 10	Customer Satisfaction
Wasted Time & Effort	Low High 1 2 3 4 5 6 7 8 9 10	Efficient & Productive
Broken Agreements	Low High 1 2 3 4 5 6 7 8 9 10	Dependable
Mistakes	Low High 1 2 3 4 5 6 7 8 9 10	Quality & Detail
Isolation	Low High 1 2 3 4 5 6 7 8 9 10	Support of Others
Disorganization	Low High 1 2 3 4 5 6 7 8 9 10	Well Organized
Low Performance	Low High 1 2 3 4 5 6 7 8 9 10	High Performance
Incomplete Tasks	Low High 1 2 3 4 5 6 7 8 9 10	Follow-Through
Static Performance	Low High 1 2 3 4 5 6 7 8 9 10	Continued Improvement

Management and Leadership Effectiveness (Based on Your Future Picture of Success)

Silo Behavior	Low High 1 2 3 4 5 6 7 8 9 10	Active Alignment
Tactical & Reactive	Low High 1 2 3 4 5 6 7 8 9 10	Strategic & Proactive
Competing Priorities	Low High 1 2 3 4 5 6 7 8 9 10	Clear Priorities
Poor Coordination	Low High 1 2 3 4 5 6 7 8 9 10	Effective Execution
Wasted Meetings	Low High 1 2 3 4 5 6 7 8 9 10	Productive Meetings
Isolated Decisions	Low High 1 2 3 4 5 6 7 8 9 10	Inclusive Decisions
Hierarchy Oriented	Low High 1 2 3 4 5 6 7 8 9 10	Engagement of All Levels
Power Driven	Low High 1 2 3 4 5 6 7 8 9 10	Results Driven

Picture of Success. She then reread her Picture of Success and started the questioning process.

As a result of recognizing her current reality, Paula realized that she had several areas in the categories of becoming indispensable, personal effectiveness, and leadership that could be improved. She was a little overwhelmed but felt good about demonstrating the courageous heart to follow through on this difficult step of the A-Loop.

PRIORITIZING YOUR CURRENT REALITY

While it is important to do a comprehensive analysis of your current reality to discover as many gaps as possible between you and your Picture of Success, this doesn't mean that you will focus on all areas surfaced at the same time. Taking on too much at once will only fragment or overwhelm you. It is much better to determine which of the gaps you have discovered are the most important for you to address at this time given your situation. Your situation includes the resources available, other goals you are currently working on, constraints that you are under, and your principles that reflect your values.

You can use the following criteria to prioritize your list of gaps surfaced by recognizing your current reality. Based on your intention, which three to five gaps, if filled, could

- move you closer to your Picture of Success within the next three to twelve months?

- be accomplished given your other commitments and competing priorities?

- be addressed with the support of others?

- be improved given financial, resource, and time constraints?

While Paula was overwhelmed after completing the process of recognizing her current reality, she calmed down completely after prioritizing her list. She discovered that if she focused on three areas needing improvement—developing her professional and technical skills, improving her communication with her teammates and management, and being more adaptable—she would make great progress on her Picture of Success. She now felt energized, more positive, more courageous, and ready to move to the next level of the A-Loop.

DARE TO REACH OUT

Now that you have completed a comprehensive analysis of your strengths and opportunities for improvement, you can look for the *linkages* and *patterns*. You may find some surprises in what you uncover. If this sounds like a tall order, I can tell you an easy way to cut the job down to size: Ask for assistance!

Second opinions are helpful, and not just for medical issues. They can be used to gain a more complete picture of your current reality. The perspective of a qualified person whom you respect can be an invaluable source of information. He or she may be able to see the big picture and offer a fresh perspective on it. Also, an outsider can see the pieces of your current reality that you may have missed. Finally, it is much easier for someone *outside* the situation to tell you the truth than it is for someone *directly* involved.

That perspective is the reason many CEOs and business professionals hire coaches and why mentoring has become such a major component in the corporate workplace.

HOW THE BEST BECOME BETTER

In Michael Jordan's biography, *Playing for Keeps*, writer David Halberstam relates a coaching story that inspired Jordan to strive harder. Dean Smith, the head coach at Jordan's alma mater (and basketball powerhouse) University of North Carolina, helped Jordan play at the next level.

At the end of Jordan's freshman year, Smith showed him a game tape and pointed out Jordan's less-than-stellar defense play. He explained the importance of being, as well as the *need* to be, a complete player. In reiterating the value of defensive skills, Smith said, "Michael, do you realize how good you can really be *defensively*?" This conversation caused Jordan to focus on that aspect of his game and become one of the best defensive players in basketball.

But Jordan's seeking out coaching perspectives didn't end when he finished college and became a professional basketball player. After his first season in the NBA, Jordan took aside Roy Williams, another one of his college coaches, and asked, "What do I need to do to work on my game?"

Considering that Jordan had just been named the NBA rookie of the year, Williams was understandably surprised and replied, "What more do you need?"

But Jordan was insistent, telling Williams, "I know you'll be honest with me—what can I do to improve myself?" So Williams suggested that he improve his jump shot. Jordan spent the summer doing exactly that, and, by the way, in the 1998 NBA championship game, Jordan's jump shot turned out to be the final and game-winning shot.

SEEK HELP FROM MORE THAN ONE PERSON

Some people think that reaching out to someone else for advice is an admission of weakness. It's just the opposite. Michael Jordan didn't hire a coach out of *weakness*; he was coming from a place of remarkable *strength*. He had as many as five coaches at one time, each working on a different aspect of his career. Whether you use professional coaches or friends, family members or teammates, religious counselors or therapists, what matters is an outside look at your situation, an observer's point of view.

There are no rules about how many coaches you can use, so find the best person to help you with *each* aspect of your life's ambitions.

Coaches don't have to last forever. They bring an expertise you don't have until you integrate the part you need. And when you've learned what you need, you move on—sometimes to the next coach. It saves you time.

SUCCESS BREEDS SUCCESS—AND YOU'VE GOT TO BE DOING SOMETHING RIGHT!

We sometimes have a tendency to focus on what we do that doesn't work. We have an inner critic who is tougher than any judge we will ever meet. We do sixty things great but make one mistake, and we kill ourselves over that one.

It is important to take the time to recognize your greatness, your uniqueness. Acknowledge your good habits so you can keep doing them. *Celebrate your strength.* If nothing else, this makes it easier to accept the part of you that you want to change. It balances things out. It gives you the self-esteem you need to roll up your sleeves and go to work. To move forward you need to see the *whole* picture and be aware of what you have working in your favor.

Finding the Right Coach

Knowing when you need a coach is one thing, but finding one is another thing altogether. Here are some tips to help you find a coach who will be effective in guiding you to achieve your goals.

1. Find someone who believes that you can achieve your goal. A believer will hold a Picture of Success, and it will be easier to see yourself in that mirror. Make sure your coach is committed to your success based on his or her belief that you can achieve it.

2. Look for a coach who has accomplished his or her own goals. Success does breed success, so find a coach who's familiar with the process of achievement. Such people will know from experience that the path isn't smooth. More important, they will have experience with the bumps in the road that need to be overcome, and they'll be able to help you get over them.

3. Choose a coach who can tell the truth without blame or judgment. When a coach's valuable observation turns into a criticism, the process quickly deteriorates into destruction rather than construction.

4. Last, select a coach who is flexible. In general, you want to work with someone who is flexible enough to modify his or her feedback, approach, and advice to meet your individual needs instead of simply taking a "cookie cutter" approach of "one size fits all."

You have now gone from ignoring your current reality to recognizing where you stand in relation to your Picture of Success. When you have prioritized your current reality, you are prepared to focus on the areas that will net you the greatest progress toward your intention. You are moving now, and you are ready to take the next step along the A-Loop toward becoming indispensable. Taking ownership is the next step after addressing your current reality and is critical for maintaining the momentum of accountability you have built.

After completing the following exercise, continue to chapter 6 and uncover the power of taking ownership.

Exercise: Recognizing Success

1. If you have not done so already, review this chapter and complete the forms for recognizing your current reality. If there are other criteria specific to your role and situation, add them to the list. Notice that it doesn't have to take a long time to recognize where you stand in relation to your Picture of Success.

2. Prioritize the top three to five areas that will give you the largest, most practical and meaningful movement toward accomplishing your Picture of Success at this time.

3. Identify your strengths based on your current success. These are not just generic strengths but those that will most contribute to your Picture of Success.

4. Finally, identify anyone who can support you on your path along the A-Loop.

You have a clear intention and a Picture of Success, so your destination is clear. Having recognized your current reality, you also know where you stand on your road to success. Now you are ready to take ownership of the part of that reality that you can do something about. While it is obvious that when we are the cause of a problem we need to fix it, there are many situations in which we are merely involved in a problem or "see" the problem. We still have the ownership to surface it, contribute to fixing it, and support others in fixing it. This is taking full dominion over the problems impacting your life. This is the step of empowerment.

*Read on to see how you can increase your influence and personal
power to be indispensable by taking ownership.*

> "Most of us can read the writing on the wall; we
> just assume it is addressed to someone else."
>
> —Ivern Ball

When you own something, you are more likely to take care
of it. You are more likely to feel responsible for it. Take a
look at the front yard of the typical rented house as
opposed to the owned one: Which is usually better cared for? The
same is true for priorities, goals, and projects. When owned, they
have a much greater chance of being achieved than when no one
has a personal stake. Once you have recognized your current reality
based on your Picture of Success, you must take ownership or
you will quickly fall down into the Victim Loop. Accepting ownership forces a personal commitment, without which your priorities, goals, and projects remain a rented house—always something
you will get to later. And that is what you will be exploring in this
chapter.

THE PROBLEM WITH AVOIDING OWNERSHIP

Ownership is the admission fee that lets you into the "solution
club." In order to jump-start the creativity to find the best solution, you have to *care*. The problem has to be yours, at least a little. If you don't want to have anything to do with it, it often sticks
to the bottom of your shoe until you pay attention to it.

When we find ourselves in difficult or challenging situations
where we have made a mistake or for which we don't have an
effective solution, we want out in the worst way. We hope it goes
away or isn't as bad as we thought. Maybe no one else will notice
and we can be relieved of the feelings of guilt, embarrassment, and
unworthiness that we might be feeling about it. Sometimes if we
could blame someone, we would—just to take off the pressure.

We'll do anything to make the challenge go away—even make a deal with God to be a better person. We don't want to own any of it. Especially if it belongs to (fill in the blank): our spouse, our boss, our child, the government, or our parents.

Well, sorry to bring the bad news. Whether you inherited the problem from your parents or previous managers or from another department in your organization, you are now part of the problem that needs fixing. We can be under the illusion that if others created the problem, it's their problem to fix. But that isn't so. As long as you are impacted by the problem, even just a little, it is your problem to fix—you own it—at least in part. And for the record, if you refuse to own any of it, you are a *victim* of it. You are unable to change a negative situation that is keeping you from being successful, feeling fulfilled, experiencing a sense of well-being if you don't own it. How do I know? Because you will think about the problem, worry about it, and bring it home with you at the end of the day. You are stuck not only with the problem but also with the feeling that you cannot do anything about it. And even if you don't have negative feelings associated with the problem, at some point the problem will get bigger and result in a failed project, a missed opportunity, or a crisis that needs fixing. As we talked about in chapter 4, not doing anything about a problem doesn't fix it. It just makes it worse.

TAKING YOUR POWER BACK

How can you possibly have a sense of power and command if you aren't in an ownership position? It is as if you are a slave and the master is your unresolved problem or challenge. You are at the mercy of it, and that doesn't feel very empowering. Some people are under the illusion that we can't take ownership for something over which we don't have complete authority. That's an all-or-nothing mind-set that doesn't work in real life. When a city experiences drought, no single person owns it completely, but we all have to save water as owners of the problem. It's *shared ownership*. When

FedEx was first created, its founder, Frederick W. Smith, asked his employees to forgo their normal salary for weeks in order to save the company. Those who could stayed, as owners of that problem, for the bigger purpose of keeping the company alive until it was successful. It was a risk. There were no guarantees, but that is what taking ownership is about: putting yourself on the line for your purpose, for sharing your gifts and making a contribution. We have seen that story replicated in more recent situations, where employees chose to take salary cuts to prevent layoffs and keep their coworkers employed. That is taking ownership of the challenging situation before them: a downturn in the economy that was threatening their business and their livelihood.

Three years ago I ended my best year in business to date. My company, IMPAQ, had solid clients with major projects creating transformational change efforts around the world and producing measurable results that we were leveraging into new sales for years to come. We were in a state of growth, and we were investing to make that happen again and enjoying life. Then the economic situation hit like a tsunami—fast and furious. Clients were canceling contracts and our proposals for new work were all on hold—permanently. Suddenly IMPAQ's revenue was down 50 percent, then 75 percent. And the remaining revenue didn't come close to paying the bills for the offices, equipment, and salaries of people supporting the organization.

It didn't take long for me to feel the weight of that situation on my head and in my heart—I was a true victim. I felt completely out of control, with no solution and watching my business, which I had built for over twenty-five years, take its last breath. I was overwhelmed not only by the challenging situation but also by added emotional strain caused in part by my inner thoughts: "It's all my fault. . . . How could God let this happen to me, when I am trying so hard? . . . I am not strong enough to handle this crisis." It didn't matter how many times I had taught the Personal Accountability Model; I was now immersed in my humanness and experiencing all of the pain and suffering that comes from victimization.

Luckily a friend of mine invited me to a workshop he was offering on leadership, which included a section on accountability. He had us participate in an exercise where, in pairs, we shared our story of victimization from the eyes of a complete victim. Since it was so fresh at the time, I shared this story and convinced my partner that in fact I was a true victim. But then my friend led the second part of the exercise, which was to tell the story as if we were completely accountable for what had happened. Of course, I didn't cause the economy to shift downward, but did I have ownership of not preparing my business to survive or thrive in an economic downturn?

I shared that before the economic downturn, I had failed to hire a financial planner to help us manage our increased funds. I had assumed that our business would continue to grow and neglected to make any contingency plan or recovery plan. And when other members of my management team had wanted to increase our expenses beyond what I was comfortable with, I had sat back in silence, never expressing my discomfort because I was embarrassed to do so. We had wanted to compete with the large consulting firms and mistakenly invested in marketing materials and image, which had cost us hundreds of thousands of dollars with little or no return. During that time, we had lost sight of our purpose: to be a boutique company with a unique service that produced measurable results unlike those of other consulting firms. In one way or another, I discovered that I had *created* the problem by spending money that should have been kept for a rainy day (and boy, did it rain), I had *promoted* it by participating in decisions that raised our overhead with little return, and I had *allowed* it to happen by not voicing my concerns when I had them.

Thus I learned yet again one of the truths of accountability. We don't just own the problems that we create. We own the ones that we promote through our communication and attitude. And we own the problems that we allow to exist and do nothing about. I also learned something that surprised me. I thought that admitting my accountability for and ownership of the downfall of my

Exercise: Taking Your Power Back

Recall a situation where you felt victimized. First describe it as if you were a total victim and there was nothing you could do to avoid it. Then describe it with total accountability. Then answer these questions:

- How did you feel in each situation?

- In which did you feel more empowered to take action?

- What are the benefits and costs of each scenario?

business would make me feel even worse and more depressed. But the opposite was true. I was completely energized to see that I had a role in the downfall, because that meant I could have a role in changing the situation. I got my power back by taking ownership. I went from feeling stuck and hopeless to feeling energized and empowered within thirty minutes of choosing to take ownership and accountability. I couldn't wait to leave the workshop and begin strategizing with my team on ways we could save the business. When you feel victimized and want to get your power back, take ownership by looking for the opportunity to learn and create a new pathway to your Picture of Success. It is very freeing.

TAKING 100 PERCENT OWNERSHIP

What I'm about to say is going to have a lot of math teachers rolling their eyes. And I was a math teacher, so I know this doesn't add up—at least not in mathematical terms. But in accountability terms it does. Each person involved in a project owns 100 percent of the project's success. If ten of us share a project, we each own 100 percent, which adds up to 1,000 percent in *accountability* land. We all need to think of ourselves as owners of a project. Whatever role you play, whatever your position in the field, whatever your level in your organization, what needs to be done needs to be done. Russell Bishop talks about this in his book, *Workarounds That Work*: "The world is full of people who are willing to do 'just so much.' . . . Then there are the 100 percent folks, those who are focused and committed to the outcome, the 'whatever it takes' people."

We *do* need to own the whole project, and at the same time we need to recognize and respect the roles of everyone involved in the project. When we accomplish that, we temporarily suspend the laws of mathematics and allow everyone to benefit from a *100 percent ownership* stake.

There was a project team I worked with for a manufacturing company. This project had a hard deadline nine months away, and the team was six weeks behind schedule. A major challenge was being short staffed and having difficulty hiring qualified people in the engineering department. When the team met and reviewed its milestones, the director of engineering would report to the rest of his team, composed of human resources, quality, manufacturing, marketing, and product development. Everyone was "involved," but not with an ownership position. They would ask good questions of the engineering director: "For the people who qualified for the position, can we offer them more salary so they don't take a job with a competitor down the street?" and "Can we develop people who are close to being ready for the position?" But these questions didn't change the results of the situation.

We applied the concept of 100 percent ownership to the situation. Instead of the director of engineering owning the shortage in his department, since all the team members would be impacted if the project failed, they all had to own the issues of staffing the engineering department. Not quite sure of the difference, they asked if we could bring up the staffing issue the same way it had been done earlier that day, and I agreed. We took a break so that they could put on their "ownership hat" and started the meeting all over again. This time, within five minutes, the quality director blurted out, "Oh, I have two friends looking for a job with the right qualifications. I will ask them to apply, since they would fit right in." The marketing person then spoke up: "I have a friend who is part of an employment agency for biotech people with the kind of qualifications we are looking for." Then the most analytical member of the team, from product development, offered her idea to transfer people from another project that was winding down to this project in start-up mode. They all loved that idea and immediately stopped the meeting to get the COO of the company in the room to discuss the new idea. The task wasn't delegated to the director of engineering; everyone on the team went to seek out the COO. Shocked by the level of demonstrated ownership, the COO immediately dropped what he was doing to join the meeting. Within one hour, we had multiple solutions, including actual people to fill the positions. Now that it was *their problem*, they showed up as owners *in the game* and produced a great result.

TAKING OWNERSHIP AT WORK

There are several places we can take greater ownership at work in order to increase our influence, our empowerment, and our indispensability. The following are common areas requiring more ownership at all levels of an organization:

- Ownership in meetings

- Ownership of surfacing and resolving issues

- Ownership of breaking down silos

- Ownership of staying focused on priorities

- Ownership of engagement at all organizational levels

- Ownership of responding to business trends

- Ownership of creating a safe work environment

Ownership in Meetings

Meetings can be used for conveying routine information or updates, sharing critical information involving change, solving problems, or

making decisions. In general, the more meetings are used for discussion to resolve problems and make decisions, the better, since
you are using the valuable resource of everyone's critical-thinking
abilities to remove barriers to success. Even when meant to be
problem solving, meetings are frequently one-way communications requiring no real level of ownership, or people come to them
with their computer, BlackBerry, or iPad to get work done while
discussions take place involving other parts of the organization.

Effective problem solving requires not only the use of various
kinds of critical thinking but also the inclusion of people who
are objective and not involved in the problem. This is why good
consultants will hire other experts to gain advice about their
own business and surgeons will not operate on their own family
members.

When you are in a meeting and the discussion is in an area
that doesn't affect you directly, it is important that you stay involved
as an "owner" to provide your critical thinking and ideas that
may impact the decision. It is also important to learn as much as
you can about the other departments or people represented in the
meeting, in order to expand your knowledge of the organization
to help you understand the impact of your decisions on others.
This knowledge will raise your influence as the person "in the
know" to make yourself indispensable.

For fifteen years I worked with an award-winning Oregon
medical center, which was one of the most accountable organizations I came into contact with. It demonstrated compassionate
accountability over and over.

I remember attending a middle-management team meeting
where the COO announced that the team had not been meeting
its budget for the last three months. Instead of pointing fingers
and placing blame on those involved in the major increase in costs
and the mistake in financial analysis, he turned his attention to
taking accountability for the problem. He said, "There is nothing
gained by finding fault with any one person here. We are all responsible in some ways for the problem, including me. Now we must

turn our attention to two things. What can we do to solve the budget crisis by taking immediate action in each of our departments, and what can we do to learn from this by creating better forecasting tools?"

After this meeting, each manager got together with his or her team and came up with a plan to cut costs and increase productivity. They didn't take the typical easy, fair approach of across-the-board cuts, which could have had a negative impact on patients and caregivers, but made reductions that would preserve the high standard of care and maintain their organizational values. Some managers took larger cuts for their departments so that patient-care areas could be sustained close to current resource levels. The focus was on finding solutions that would be best for the entire organization.

Within three months the organization was back on track. Morale improved as they worked together to resolve this crisis. They also developed more sophisticated financial systems to track results on a monthly basis. The focus on *finding solutions* and the *compassion* that underlined their actions are what allowed them to win and come out of this situation in better shape than they had been in the first place. Over the years it has been during breakdowns and crises that they have discovered their true strength.

Ownership of Surfacing and Resolving Issues

Some of the biggest breakdowns that occur in organizations stem from unresolved issues that have plagued the organization for years, if not decades. They represent "the way things are done in this organization," even though they don't work. Examples are the lack of coordination between two departments that are operating as silos or a procedure/policy that was put in place to solve a problem that existed twenty years ago but no longer does. The net result is wasted time, energy, and resources—all of which, these days, an organization can't afford.

While people tend to notice these kinds of problems and surface them in the hallway or lunchroom with others who agree and can commiserate with one another to feel better, nothing is getting solved. Taking ownership means that you are willing to surface the problem to the people who can change it, regardless of where in the organization that might be, and come to them with possible solutions or ways to get to a solution. You are not just another complainer but someone who is known for taking any problem toward resolution. It doesn't mean that you will always be successful. All indispensable people have their failings or false starts, but eventually they are viewed as positive instigators of change and improvement.

Ownership of Breaking Down Silos

It's easy to define success in terms of our job or our team. In fact, in most organizations we are compensated based on our individual performance. However, that is a fast track to becoming dispensable and dropping down into the Victim Loop. Silos are a plague in most organizations because they result in low performance, poor use of resources, breakdown of trust and collaboration, poor customer service, and delayed projects costing millions of dollars.

It is essential for middle managers to get out of their functional silos to coordinate and collaborate effectively across the organization, and resolve cross-functional challenges. However, it is also important for individuals and teams at all levels of the organization to ensure organizational success over functional or personal success.

Ownership of Staying Focused on Priorities

One of the greatest challenges negatively impacting performance and morale is the inability to stay focused on priorities. The problem is simple. When everything is a top priority, nothing is a priority. And there is nothing worse than changing priorities on a daily basis based on whims and desires as opposed to what is absolutely necessary for success. The problems of the "priority of the week" and priorities being moving targets are based on the illusion that naming something a priority assures that it will get done. Rotating priorities mean that you are starting something and not completing it before you move on to something else. This only builds a pile of uncompleted priorities robbing you of your resources, time, and energy.

One of the most important reasons to focus on only a few priorities is that you can dedicate enough resources to complete those priorities so that you can add new priorities in their place. Without completing some priorities before you bring on new ones, you will always run out of resources and develop competing priorities. The result is fragmentation, frustration, chaos, and burnout.

Ownership of Engagement at All Organizational Levels

The greatest asset and strength of any organization is its human capital, not just as bodies taking up space or doing their jobs, but also as people solving problems and contributing to improvement. In a world that is constantly improving quality, efficiency, and service, improvement is not a luxury or optional. Unfortunately, either we don't solicit the ideas of others (whether it be other departments or other organizational levels) who may have valuable insights and ideas or we create an environment of "fear of retribution" for saying anything less than positive. While supervisors must do their best to create an open and safe environment for people to share their ideas, it is also the responsibility of employees to share their ideas in the direction of making the organization better rather than being only self-serving. They must also actively engage themselves for the betterment of the organization and their team. When supervisors and employees do that, they create a positive "buzz" that is fun, high performing, and successful.

Ownership of Responding to Business Trends

No organization operates in a vacuum. Each organization is impacted by technological advancements, economic changes, societal trends, government regulation, and competition. While often viewed as an executive role, it is critical for everyone in the organization to be aware of business and industry trends. Why? Because if you want to stay in business or remain employed (or employable), you must respond to the world around you; otherwise you become obsolete. This is one of the most critical responsibilities for those becoming indispensable and taking accountability for their future. Your customers and the changing world define responsiveness, quality, productivity, and creativity. Your job, regardless of position, is to translate changing business trends into your personal and professional development to be as adaptable as possible.

Exercise: Increasing Your Ownership at Work

Take a few minutes to explore ways in which you can take more ownership in your organization. Answer the first question thinking about your role on your team and your job. Then answer the second question thinking about how you can contribute to your organization in a different and more expanded way.

1. In which of the functions you are involved in (such as meetings, projects, and improvement efforts) can you contribute more? What would you be doing differently to participate in those activities playing a "big game" rather than a comfortable "small game"?

2. Based on your general role in the organization, what could you be doing differently to demonstrate a higher level of ownership? What could you be doing to have a greater positive influence on others and on the organization's success?

Ownership of Creating a Safe Work Environment

Nobody wins and everybody loses when someone gets hurt on the job. It is everyone's responsibility to ensure a safe work environment. First, managers must establish safety as the number one priority. However, this goes beyond lip service, posters, and rule books. This must be reinforced when there is a choice between safety and productivity. Productivity can never be more important than keeping someone out of harm's way. At the same time, safety behavior must be coached by supervisors on the line and in the field; simply documenting someone's lack of safety is not a solution. Finally, every employee, regardless of level or position, must look out for every other employee's safety and be willing to challenge anyone who is not abiding by safety procedures, reminding that person to slow down and act in a fully safe manner. Safety is one area where everyone can gain practice increasing their level of accountability and indispensability—their value to others.

BEWARE: OWNERSHIP TRAPS

Sometimes, when there are several contributors to a situation, people can get sidetracked by measuring their *share* of ownership. When this happens, measuring ownership can quickly become a roadblock to success. There are three traps to watch for: power, martyrdom, and denial/blame.

The Power Trap

This trap springs up when someone declares ownership in order to take control over others. This is often witnessed when one department leader wants to have control over other departments or to compete against others for resources rather than finding the optimal balance of resources for everyone's success.

The Martyrdom Trap

This trap springs up when we take *all the blame* for a situation. The martyrdom trap takes place when we are overresponsible for situations and preventing others involved to learn from their involvement. A director in a manufacturing plant got into the martyrdom trap and as a result, his team became dependent on him for their motivation and solving problems. As a result, internal customers weren't getting served. Even though the manager demonstrated personal accountability, upper management removed him from his management position, because he wasn't developing his team.

The Denial/Blame Trap

This one springs up whenever someone uses an ownership "percentage game" to *sidestep* accountability. Imagine two drivers pulling out of their parking spots at a shopping mall and reaching the same place at the same time resulting in a collision. This accident was caused by the carelessness *of both* drivers. But suddenly one driver jumps out of his car, points his finger at the other driver, and says she is *more* to blame than he is. This is a direct attempt to deny ownership.

In each of these traps, ownership is inappropriate, and there's either too much or not enough. It leaves one or both participants frustrated, angry, or helpless.

Ownership increases your involvement. It gives you the impetus to do your very best. It opens the flow of creativity and allows you to access an intuition and energy that only come if you care, if you are involved. You are getting out of the Victim Loop and using accountability to own more of the outcome than you knew was yours to own.

TAKING OWNERSHIP DURING TRANSITION

One of the most challenging times for people is when they are in transition out of a job and either jobless or moving to another job. In this situation, you may be angry, hurt, and discouraged or optimistic, excited, and relieved. Regardless, you may be feeling a sense of fear about the new circumstances you will be thrown into

How One Woman Turned a Personal Loss into a Public Crusade

Ordinary people can accomplish extraordinary things when they make a situation their own. Candy Lightner's response to the tragic death of her thirteen-year-old daughter, Cari, is a poignant example. In 1980 a drunken driver, who had been released on bail after a hit-and-run accident just two days earlier, killed Cari. The driver had multiple DUI accidents and convictions on his record, and yet he was allowed to keep his license.

The grief and anger that Lightner experienced in response to her daughter's death were not unusual, but the way she chose to deal with her loss was. "I promised myself on the day of Cari's death that I would fight to make this needless homicide count for something in the years ahead," she wrote in her book, *Giving Sorrow Words.*

A few days after her daughter's funeral, Lightner met with a group of friends, and the idea for MADD, Mothers Against Drunk Driving, was born. Lightner had taken ownership of an ambitious project—she planned to prevent some of the tens of thousands of deaths caused by drunk driving each year. In the two decades since, MADD has been instrumental in reducing alcohol-related traffic deaths by 38 percent, and *more than 138,000 lives have been saved.* On its twentieth anniversary, MADD had three million members and more than six hundred local chapters throughout North America.

It is worth asking what might have happened if Candy Lightner had not taken a solution-oriented approach to Cari's death and instead had become mired in the situation itself. She could have succumbed to the grief and depression that naturally follow the death of a loved one. Or she could have devoted her energy to ensuring that the driver was punished, and she might never have founded MADD.

For more information about MADD, go to www.MADD .org.

as a result of the transition. It is not uncommon for people to disengage from their current job, knowing that it no longer matters for their next review or compensation discussion. And it's even worse if you know that there may be a downsize coming or a restructuring about to be implemented. You may say, "Maybe I should start looking now for a new job." While it may be prudent to look for a new job, it is a terrible mistake to disconnect from being your best in the current job you are in for any reason—even being laid off or getting a new job.

Being indispensable doesn't start and stop with whatever job you are currently in. It is a lasting state based on the value you represent to others. And even if you leave an organization, there is no reason to diminish your value. If anything, it is better to provide even more value as a way to let the employer know what it will be missing in your absence.

Do you think a famous comedian like Robin Williams or a famous musician like Stevie Wonder performs with less commitment when he is playing a concert for charity than when he is playing a concert that is a sellout where he earns millions? No. Regardless of the situation, he is giving his performance 100 percent. Whether she is in transition, has been on the job for twenty-five years, or is just starting out, the accountable and indispensable person gives her performance 100 percent—she cares about her impact on others and the value others receive.

Taking ownership requires courage, and the reward is empowerment. Once you take ownership, problems are no longer running you. You are in command of them, even though they're not

Exercise: From Victim to Accountability and Taking Charge

Make a list of situations where you have felt victimized, where you have felt you had nothing to do with a problem that arose. Something just "happened" to you. Then relook at each situation and find ways to take more ownership of your part in the problem.

yet solved. Following the path of the A-Loop, you have now recognized and owned your role in improvement and in achieving your
Picture of Success. You are about to discover, in the next chapter,
the best-kept secret in the voyage toward the freedom that comes
from being accountable and indispensable: self-forgiveness.

CHAPTER 7:
GAINING STRENGTH THROUGH FORGIVENESS

After recognizing your current state and taking ownership, you are ready for the next step in the Accountability Loop: overcoming the judgments you have picked up along the way. Judgments are like a bag of rocks you are carrying over your shoulders. It weighs you down as you move forward toward achieving your Picture of Success. Removing the barriers associated with guilt, resentment, disappointment, and discouragement provides the strength necessary to move on in the A-Loop. The most indispensable and accountable people make mistakes, but their resilience begins with forgiveness and releasing the negativity of human error that plagues us all. How do you overcome the *relentless attacks you get from your inner critic? How do you forgive without missing the learning opportunities that come from mistakes? These questions and others will be answered as they relate to becoming indispensable.*

> "The old law of 'an eye for an eye' leaves everybody blind."
>
> —Martin Luther King Jr.

O nce you take ownership, you've opened up the can of criticism. After all, who wants to be put on the line and attacked by others or, worse, by themselves? Nobody. So on the heels of ownership we may get cold feet and want to run away by deflecting, hiding, ignoring, or using any other method to keep the fingers from pointing at us. No matter how big or small, external or internal, criticism is hard to bear. It would be simpler to go back to the old way of finding excuses or blaming others. However, when you run away, the only place you can go is down into the Victim Loop. In this chapter we will take a fresh look at an essential and too often ignored step for being and staying accountable: forgiveness. Whether directed at others or ourselves, forgiveness is the way out of this self-defeating cycle.

LET'S GET REAL—THE HUMAN FACTOR

No matter how dedicated you are to being accountable, how much you try to keep all of your commitments and agreements, and how well you have demonstrated accountability in the past, you will drop the ball. You will make mistakes, not keep a commitment to your boss, and probably even not keep an agreement you made with yourself. It's bound to happen. This does not mean you are not being accountable, any more than Michael Jordan missing a game-winning shot made him unaccountable. Accountability is *not* about being perfect!

The first thing you are accountable for is being human. We can count on your being human and, as such, making mistakes like every other human being. No matter the length of your "winning" streak, at some point your humanness will show up and you will make mistakes or fail. It is inevitable. And if you are making yourself indispensable, you are pushing the envelope on the status quo, taking calculated risks, and inventing new pathways to higher levels of excellence. You are bound to make mistakes on that path, and that can't determine your level of accountability.

FORGIVENESS—THE MISSING KEY
TO TRUE ACCOUNTABILITY

True accountability is not based on theoretical models or concepts of perfection where you are expected to keep every agreement and commitment—that is a nicely packaged fantasy. True accountability has to include our humanness. But if the measure of accountability isn't the perfect manner in which you keep every commitment and agreement, what is it?

The measure of accountability is based more on how you handle mistakes, mishaps, and breakdowns than on getting everything right all the time. It's about how fast you pick yourself up when you fall; how quickly you correct a mistake that you made; how well you make up for a broken commitment in order to ensure that little or no harm comes to your customer, family member, or friend. It's easy to be accountable when everything is going your way or when you tell someone else to just do it. But in the real world, there are many challenges that come our way that we can't control, and how we anticipate them and adapt when they do surface determines our effectiveness and our accountability.

The reason forgiveness is the overlooked but critical key to accountability is that when you don't forgive, you end up in either the blame game of making a problem someone else's fault or the excuses game of finding all of the reasons you shouldn't be blamed for the breakdown or inadequacy. This puts you back in the self-defeating Victim Loop and never solves or remedies the breakdown. You are stuck with the problem. The sooner you forgive the humanness involved in any breakdown or inadequacy, the faster you move back to the A-Loop, where you can focus on resolving the problem and making improvement. And that is your only way to eventual success. Forgiveness is demonstrated by your actions to remedy the situation, not your words of apology.

> "I've missed more than nine thousand shots in my career. I've lost almost three hundred games. Twenty-six times I've been trusted to take the game winning shot and missed. I've failed over and over and over again in my life. And that is why I succeed."
>
> —Michael Jordan

SAYING "I'M SORRY" DOESN'T MEAN FORGIVENESS

I often hear the question "Isn't forgiveness a way out of being accountable?" I have heard this from organizations that "didn't believe in forgiveness, because they didn't want to give people permission to make mistakes." Forgiveness isn't about letting people off the hook for their commitments or condoning inappropriate behavior, bad communication, or actions that produce negative results. True forgiveness involves rectifying a situation that is off track from the commitment made. Saying "I'm sorry" doesn't accomplish that. If there is something to correct, action to do so must accompany your words of apology. And so often what we witness instead is a person who says "I'm sorry" but continues to make the same error over and over again. Maybe it's repeatedly showing up late to meetings or not keeping to the committed schedule or expressing unbridled anger. Saying "I'm sorry" doesn't cut it.

The other day I needed to purchase a white shirt to wear with my suit for a special event that night. I called a store where I regularly buy my shirts to make sure it had one available in my size. The clerk, Tony, assured me that it would be there when I arrived in a couple of hours. When I got to the store, Tony gave me the bad news. He had been mistaken, and he apologized profusely.

But his apology didn't solve my problem, and he knew it. Tony immediately got on the phone and called another store to find the shirt I wanted in my size. He paid a courier to pick up the shirt and get it to me within the hour. Yes, it cost me an extra hour, but at least I got the shirt without needing to run around the city trying to find it. Tony was being accountable. And his apology meant something, because he did his best to remedy the situation. Even when you are doing your best, you will make mistakes and have breakdowns.

ACCOUNTABLE DELEGATION AND AGREEMENTS

How often do you ask someone for a commitment or agreement and get a response of yes that really means no? You may even ask the person again if he is sure, and he will look at you straight in the eyes and say, "Yes, I am sure." But what he really means is "Yes, I am committed, unless something else comes up that is more important." This is a prescription for breakdown and failure, because there will always be something coming up that is more important, a crisis to address or some act of nature—all resulting in blame, excuses, or forgiveness.

Whether delegating to someone down your line of authority or making an agreement with someone who doesn't report to you in the chain of command, the process of establishing an accountable commitment is the same. Accountable commitments require three steps: clear outcomes, identification of obstacles to success, and proactive recovery plans.

Step #1: Agreeing on Outcomes Instead of Tasks

The most common practice for delegation is to delegate tasks or get agreement from coworkers to take on a task as a support for accomplishing organizational goals. Unfortunately, the person can complete the task delegated or agreed upon, but not meet desired expectations from that task resulting in disappointment and frustration on the part of both parties. Of course, if you delegate a task and want to ensure success, then the most common approach is to micromanage the person, which results in frustration and resentment. In either case, both parties lose—the delegator and the person taking on the task.

Instead of delegating or getting agreements to tasks, it is more effective to delegate desired outcomes for what you are expecting. Then, there is less interpretation and more clarity about the criteria for success that is being requested. Besides, would you prefer someone to be accountable for doing a task or accomplishing a result? It is important for managers and direct reports alike to ensure understanding of the desired outcome before delegating or accepting responsibility for completing a task.

Step #2: Identifying Obstacles to Success

While you may think you have a clear agreement now that you have commitment to the desired outcome instead of to the task, you are still very vulnerable to breakdown and surprises. In our desire to please others and our general good intentions, we can commit to doing something that we don't have a chance of completing. We want to. We intend to. We may even be excited about this new opportunity. But that doesn't mean that in reality, given competing priorities or the situation we are in, we will be able to keep the commitment. And many times when we are asked to do something, we don't take the time to think it through—it becomes an emotional response to say yes, because we really want to help and to be seen as competent.

Since your success depends on other people's effectiveness, you certainly don't want to leave it up to chance whether someone you are depending on keeps their commitment. Before you accept the commitment as an accountable agreement, you must ask the person, "What breakdowns might take place that will keep you from being successful in achieving the agreed-upon desired outcome?"

Asking about potential breakdowns allows the person who is

making the commitment to slow down their process and think about the commitment they are making to ensure it is a valid agreement. And it allows you to review the potential breakdowns to determine if it is worth the risk of your desired outcome to give them the assignment or would be better to give it to someone else. Maybe you can remedy some of the potential breakdowns before they occur.

This step of identifying potential breakdowns prevents surprises. The potential breakdowns exist whether you are aware of them or not. At least knowing them provides you options. Not knowing them results in a surprise when the person falls prey to a hidden obstacle. But you are not done yet. There is one more step in creating an accountable agreement.

Step #3: Proactive Recovery Plans

The key to accountability is fast recovery when a breakdown occurs—the faster, the better. Unfortunately, when breakdowns occur it can surprise us, resulting in crisis and shock. And when in shock or crisis, we are not necessarily thinking clearly or creatively to find the best solution. We look for quick fixes to remedy a problem that is already in motion. Proactive Recovery Plans anticipate breakdowns *before* they happen. We develop next steps for resolving those breakdowns, even if we don't have complete solutions. Proactive recovery helps you to develop next steps, which may be as simple as "Let me know if this breakdown shows up" or "Contact this person on the team if this problem surfaces."

Without Proactive Recovery Plans, the tendency is to determine the source of the problem, which generally results in finding someone to blame, which leads into the Victim Loop. Of course the response from the person being blamed is to give excuses for the breakdown. And while you might want to debate the validity of the excuses, the problem is that even if the excuses are valid, they don't achieve the desired outcome. The net result is still failure. Proactive Recovery Plans are the best way to ensure success, since it prepares you for adapting to change.

HOLDING OTHERS ACCOUNTABLE WITH FORGIVENESS

No matter how well we set up accountable agreements using the strategy above, as human beings people will break commitments from time to time. Unfortunately, when others we depend on don't keep their commitments, it can impact our own ability to achieve our commitments and keep our agreements. So while this book is focused on making yourself indispensable and increasing your level of personal accountability, it is essential to develop the skill of holding others accountable in a supportive manner.

Forgiveness doesn't mean ignoring broken agreements. We must learn the most difficult skill of being accountable: holding others accountable while still taking ownership of how we contributed to the breakdown. Effectively holding others accountable is not blaming people for making a mistake, since that takes us down the Victim Loop. Besides, no positive result comes from pointing the finger at the person causing a breakdown. We may feel better, but we have solved nothing. So what does it mean to hold others accountable without blame? Before we answer that question, let's explore the other three common traps people fall into when holding others accountable that result in a direct flight back into the Victim Loop.

Trap #1: Gossip—Breaking Down Trust

Instead of confronting the person who is causing the problem, it is much easier to talk negatively about this person to our friends and associates. That way we can avoid confrontation. Besides, we can gain a lot of influence by getting others to take our side in a conflict. And the perpetrator isn't there to defend himself, so we can say whatever we want in presenting our side of the story.

The problem with gossip is that it causes hurt feelings and breaks down trust. It's a lose-lose situation for the person being gossiped about. If they provide their side of the story, they will be viewed as defensive. If they say nothing, they will be viewed as condoning the gossiper's story. Ultimately, gossiping breaks down trust, as I witnessed with a group of ten managers I worked with several years ago. They were a very tight group and, using IMPAQ's Team Relationship Assessment, scored 6.25 out of 7 on demonstrating mutual trust. The leader of the team hired a new eleventh person to the team who, it was later discovered, was into the gossiping game. Within six months, conflicts in the group were on the rise. When I gave the same team the same Team Relationship Assessment, their new score on trust was 2.75 out of 7—representing a huge drop in trust. It was easy to identify the source of the problem, given that the only change to the team in the last six months was the new player. That person was dropped from the team, and the leader decided not to replace her. So the team was now back to its original ten members. However, six months later, when they took the same Team Relationship Assessment, they scored only 4 on trust. Even after two years of working together, the same ten team members never rebuilt the trust they had before the gossiper contaminated their team. Gossiping is a deadly way to hold others accountable, since it erodes trust.

Trap #2: Ignore—Creating Mediocrity

One of the easiest and most popular ways to deal with a broken commitment or agreement is to ignore it. We just don't have time to deal with this or we have more important things to take care of. The problem with ignoring a problem is that it will get bigger over time. In addition, ignoring broken commitments results in mediocrity. Whatever low level of performance, behavior, or communication you are ignoring becomes the new standard.

Trap #3: Rescue—Fostering Victimization

One of the most effective ways to hold others accountable when they are not getting the job done is to do it for them. At least in this response you can achieve a successful outcome. And on occasion this is necessary in any team environment. As a regular pattern, however, it is a very dangerous strategy. But it is also a very seductive approach, since there are so many benefits for the person doing the rescuing. You get to be the hero, saving the day for the team or organization. You get to demonstrate that you are more competent than the others on the team, since you got the job done. If you were promoted over others on the team, they now know why you deserve that position. But with all those wonderful accolades you are now doing other people's jobs and either not getting your own job done or spending all hours of the night and weekends doing double work. And if you are doing others' jobs for them, they are not getting developed to do their jobs on their own, meaning there is no end to this process in sight. You are truly trapped!

While becoming aware of ineffective methods of holding others accountable is helpful, it is even more important to have a clear process for holding others accountable in a way that is supportive, incorporates forgiveness, and focuses on achieving results. You can tell when you have succeeded in holding others accountable— everyone's accountability, including yours, increases, and higher results are achieved. By following the process provided below in five simple (not always easy) steps, you can become a master at holding yourself and others accountable.

FIVE STEPS FOR HOLDING OTHERS ACCOUNTABLE

Holding others accountable isn't about blaming anyone or finding fault. The purpose of holding others accountable is to solve problems, increase effectiveness, and improve communication. Ultimately, when you are adding to the value of others' efforts and raising the standard of performance, you are making yourself indispensable.

Step #1: Review the Commitment or Agreement

The first step involves surfacing the original commitment or agreement. It is the starting place, since a common understanding of the agreement is necessary for keeping it. Obviously, if the commitment is to complete a task, there is lots of room for misunderstanding. But if the agreement is to achieve a desired outcome or Picture of Success, then you are clear on expectations and the criteria for success. This is typically not an emotionally based discussion—it is a factual perception check on the level of clarity of the original agreement. In one case the agreement was to produce a plan "right away." One person viewed "right away" as three business days, while the other viewed "right away" as within one day. Sometimes reviewing the agreement solves the breakdown by clearing up confusion. But if it doesn't, you are now ready for step #2.

Step #2: Acknowledge the Situation Without Judgment

This is a very important step that requires skill to contain the conversation. In this step, you are acknowledging the broken commitment without blame or explanation. In other words, if you were supposed to be given information by Monday at noon and it is 1:00 P.M. and you haven't received the information, acknowledging the situation sounds like this: "We had an agreement that you were to get me information by Monday at noon, and I don't have it." It is a simple reporting of the facts and only the facts! It is not "Why didn't you get me this information on time?" or "You can't be trusted, since you failed again to get me information by Monday at noon, which was your commitment." Those are judgmental statements that the person can defend or deflect by blaming someone or something else.

It is possible that when you acknowledge the situation just as it is, the person might respond with excuses for why they didn't complete the commitment as it was made. As much as possible, you want to avoid getting caught in the defend-attack-defend cycle. It becomes a never-ending and pointless conversation, since all of the excuses in the world, valid or not, won't achieve a successful outcome. All you are looking for is an agreement that the commitment wasn't kept, with no blame attached. Now you are prepared for the most important step in the process.

Step #3: Support the Person in Taking Accountability

While support may seem like a "soft" approach, it is the only way to raise accountability and keep the pressure on someone to perform. However, the catch is that support *cannot* include rescue. The specific question for this step is "How can I support you in you keeping your commitment and resolving any challenges before you?" In the world of elite sports and performing arts, when someone has difficulty with his performance, teammates will offer to practice with him until he gets it right. They don't ignore, avoid, or blame him for not performing. They work with him to help him be the best he can be. Support in the workplace involves brainstorming solutions and sharing resources creatively and can even include helping the person, as long as you aren't doing the job for him. You know this step is being executed effectively when the discussion is all about solutions.

Step #4: Recommitment, Recovery Plan, and Follow-through

Based on the results of step #3, it is time to establish new commitments to both the outcome being accomplished and the actions that will represent a "do differently" approach to achieving success. While you may think you have the new solution that is going to work, you still need to brainstorm possible breakdowns and agree on the recovery plans to address them. This step isn't complete until you establish an agreed-upon follow-up schedule to make sure everything is on track.

Step #5: Persevere When All Else Fails

No matter how effectively you create accountable agreements and hold others accountable, there will be individuals who just don't want to be accountable. That's okay. You actually repeat the process by returning to step #1. While it appears to be repetitive, in actuality each round raises the stakes on being accountable. Generally you will find that on the second or third round, even the most resistant individual will cooperate with the process of moving to the next level of accountability.

There was one person, Dave, on Chris's team whose failures to keep his commitments on the project impacted several other team members. Chris used to get really upset with Dave and embarrass him in front of others to get his attention. But it never worked. Now he applied the accountability process and got the team involved in step #3 to brainstorm options for resolving the obstacles that were keeping Dave from achieving results. Dave responded to his teammates' input and began hitting his target schedule. When he was asked a few months later about his experience of being held accountable in this new approach, his comments were profound and clear: "When I was being yelled at and embarrassed in front of my team, it was easier for me to blame Chris as a bad leader and manager for his style. But when he changed his approach to focusing on results and supporting me to achieve those results, there was no place to hide. How could I resist support? And when my teammates got involved, the stakes went up again. Now everyone was looking at my performance and part of my recovery plan. I had to perform."

I FORGIVE YOU, AND YOU'RE FIRED

I don't have to blame you or make you wrong to determine that you may not fit in this organization. Not everyone is a fit in every organization, and that doesn't make them wrong or bad. But it doesn't mean that they should stay and be unsuccessful. I believe that everyone fits somewhere. And one's fit could change over time.

Yolanda was a member of my team for three years. Suddenly I noticed that her performance was slipping. I provided coaching, holding her accountable, but she didn't respond. Finally I had a heart-to-heart talk with her about her goals and how she was doing working for me. She responded, "While I love the work and being part of the IMPAQ team, I don't like working with groups as much as I like individual coaching." Instead of blaming Yolanda for her unsatisfactory performance, I suggested that she find a job with another consulting group that provided more coaching to its clients than we did at that time. She was thrilled at the idea and quickly got a job with another firm.

What if Yolanda hadn't wanted to leave my organization? Then I would have continued to hold her accountable and we would have started a corrective-action program until either she

turned around and performed well again or we let her go because
the fit wasn't there. But in no case would it have been necessary to
stand against Yolanda. It is possible to preserve the dignity of each
individual even though she may need to leave your organization.

FORGIVENESS: THE CORE COMPETENCY
FOR HIGHLY SUCCESSFUL INDIVIDUALS

Forgiveness is underrated as "soft" when in fact it takes great
strength and is an essential ingredient for anyone with sustainable
success. The issue is simple: When you come across a breakdown,
an unexpected mishap, or some other problem generated by you
or someone else, the only way to get past it is to focus on solutions. As long as you are focusing on the problem, you aren't coming up with solutions. Whether you are complaining that something
isn't good or blaming someone else for a breakdown, you aren't
doing anything to solve the issue. Therefore, you are stuck in the
Victim Loop—forever, until you apply forgiveness and move on!

The tricky part of forgiveness is that we generally think it applies
to other people when they let us down, break a commitment, or
hurt us in some way. But the biggest challenge with forgiveness is
when we let ourselves down. When we blow the presentation that
we practiced so hard to get right. When we study so hard for the
test and still end up with a C or worse. And when we do our best
to communicate effectively only to find others confused by our
message. Any one of these situations can result in a tailspin of self-
judgment—blaming ourselves. "I'm just not smart enough, strong
enough, disciplined enough, good enough," you might be saying
to yourself. "I am too fat, too nice, too timid, too shy, or too
loud." You may be predicting your future with self-judgmental
comments like "I will never make it or be a success," "I just don't
have the skills or looks to be successful," or "They will never give
me a break or value my strengths." You are in a downward spiral
of self-doubt and hopelessness, and this is no way to resolve the
issue. The people succeeding make the same mistakes you do, but
they skip self-judgment and move right to corrective learning and

Letting Go: A Zen Tale

A young monk was traveling with an older monk when they came to a river. On the bank was an attractive, finely clothed young woman who could not cross the river without ruining her gown. The young monk heeded his vows to avoid contact with the opposite sex, and he looked away. But his elder walked directly to the woman and offered his help. He carried her across the muddy river and put her down. After she thanked him, the woman and the monks parted ways.

The young monk was shocked by the elder's behavior, and he silently stewed about it until, hours later, he could not hold his tongue any longer. "How could you do that?" he complained. "It is a violation to even look at a woman, and you spoke with her. You carried her!"

The older monk thought about his young companion's criticism and, smiling, he replied, "I put her down on the other side of the river hours ago, but you are still carrying her."

action. They don't waste time in self-pity or self-recrimination. They are focused only on solving the challenges before them. It takes strength, discipline, and clarity of purpose.

Whether it's a judgment against someone else or a judgment against yourself, it is in the past and it is holding you back. No matter how much you think you are right about the mistake, inadequacy, or breakdown, there is nothing you can do about it and it is time to let it go, much like the monk in the story. Take a deep breath, and as you let your breath out, allow the guilt, resentment, disappointment, and discouragement to go with it. Then quickly focus on right now . . . your next breath. And notice how you feel without carrying the rocks of judgment on your back.

DEVELOPING THE STRENGTH TO FORGIVE

You might think that others don't have self-defeating thoughts, since they have such great track records of success behind their names. But this couldn't be further from the truth. Before they were successful, they had the same self-doubt, self-judgment, and negative thinking that you experience. Everyone at every level has gone into doubt at some time in his life. The difference is that they developed the strength and discipline to not get caught in that kind of negative thinking. And that is why it takes great skill and strength to apply forgiveness in a way that focuses you on solutions rather than on giving up.

FORGIVENESS IS UNIVERSAL

To practice the kind of forgiveness I talk about in this book, you can be a member of any religion, any faith, or any spiritual practice, or you can have no faith at all. You don't need to go to a specific place of worship, and there's no need for prayer or sacred assemblies. This forgiveness gets practiced *by* you, *for* you. It is practical, daily, pragmatic. You can do it alone, accompanied by a coach, or with a group of friends. You can be at work, at home, or in nature. It can take two minutes or be a process of an hour or more. However you want to do it, it is your choice. What matters is to do it. Just that.

The purpose of forgiveness is to let go of the baggage you don't need. The point here is not to address whether you were right, whether the other person should be punished, or whether he or she deserves to be forgiven. Each person has his or her unique value system, and it would be impossible to address all of them here. What matters is that forgiveness is done for your own benefit. In simple terms, you are happier when you are able to forgive. You become more productive when you forgive. You become more creative in solving problems. You become more understanding, which is necessary for working with others on your team. You become more confident when you forgive, knowing that you aren't stuck with your past and soon will be developing your better future. Forgiveness represents taking the high road—the accountable road.

THE MOST POWERFUL FORGIVENESS
TOOL—SELF-FORGIVENESS

When I was studying for my master's degree in applied psychology at the University of Santa Monica (USM), I learned the process of self-forgiveness. This is now taught by the president and the chief academic officer of USM, Drs. Ron and Mary Hulnick, in their best-selling book, *Loyalty to Your Soul*. The process is simple, but the impact is huge. It is based on the concept that given that we are human, we will make mistakes. We don't need to forgive the fact that we made a mistake any more than we need to forgive ourselves for coughing. Making mistakes is natural, normal, and something we do from the moment we are born to the day we die. We may not like making mistakes, but I am not fond of coughing either.

So if we aren't forgiving the mistake we made, what are we forgiving? We are forgiving the judgment we placed against ourselves for the mistake we made. Why would we treat ourselves so poorly when it is just our humanness that showed up, especially when it really doesn't help us to correct the mistake or prevent us from making mistakes in the future? Self-forgiveness is used to eliminate the suffering you are inflicting on yourself unnecessarily, which has a negative impact on your work, your relationships, and your personal life.

The technique of self-forgiveness begins with identifying the judgment: "I'm not a good enough manager"; "I'm not organized enough"; "I'm not an effective communicator"; or "I'm not a good enough parent." Then you apply the following sentence, which you say to yourself with as much caring and compassion as you can muster: "I forgive myself for judging myself for _____." (Insert the judgment in the blank space.)

And you repeat this sentence for each and every judgment you hear yourself say in the privacy of your own head.

APPLYING THE TOOL OF SELF-FORGIVENESS AT WORK

A few years ago I was coaching Gary, one of my associates, who had to make an eight-hour presentation to a group of managers on Accountable Performance Coaching—a topic he hadn't presented on before. It was a grueling three hours of coaching and course correction. After forty-five minutes he asked me for a break so that he could use the tool of "self-forgiveness." He said he was starting to get down on himself and couldn't focus on learning. Gary took a few minutes to forgive himself for judging himself for not learning fast enough. He said, "I forgive myself for judging myself for not being a good enough consultant. I forgive myself for judging myself for not being dynamic and confident enough. I forgive myself for judging myself as not being smart enough." He kept on for about five minutes, sharing self-forgiveness for all the different judgments that had entered his mind.

When he came back, he said, "Okay, I'm ready for more corrective feedback." The technique had worked. Gary was calm, open, and ready to hear more feedback on the next section of the training program.

Although I knew this technique was powerful for neutralizing self-judgment, I had never thought of using it at work. It turned out to be the most effective way to stay in the learning process rather than getting sidetracked by my inner critical voice. The recovery was fast, and the faster, the better. Gary took three more breaks to do more self-forgiveness before we were finished. The next week he gave a fantastic presentation to a group of highly trained managers. The participants evaluated his presentation with excellent scores, and his presentation led to five additional training programs. Gary clearly demonstrated the power of self-forgiveness.

THE PROCESS OF FORGIVING, LETTING GO, AND MOVING ON

It's not enough to forgive the judgments, because you can create them all over again unless you are willing to let go of them. What does it mean to let them go? Let them go to the universe, to God, to the air you breathe, to nature anywhere but inside of you. Holding on to judgment has no purpose. So once you forgive, let it go. And to solidify letting it go, move on to your future. Remind yourself of your intention to be a top performer, a top communicator, a wonderful spouse, teammate, or partner. Make that your focus, and start over again on your path to achieving success.

Deborah, the struggling entrepreneur, needed to apply self-forgiveness to let go of her failure as a businesswoman and begin again. She was carrying with her in her mind the picture of failure and all of the judgments that went with it. She judged herself for being a bad businesswoman, a poor leader, and a terrible salesperson and for mismanaging her finances. There was no way for her to have a second chance at her new business if she was stuck thinking about her past mistakes. Deborah not only went through the "self-forgiveness" process, but she also let go of her past, so that she could focus on her new future. Moving on for Deborah meant creating her new Picture of Success and beginning to act on it through the volunteer service work she did to utilize her core gifts and strengths.

FORGIVENESS IS NOT THE CLOSING ACT

One of the biggest problems with forgiveness is the idea that once you ask for forgiveness, all can be forgotten, or that it's a remedy for the previous breakdown. Saying you're sorry and gaining or giving forgiveness is *never* the *end* of the process. Why? Because without learning and doing something differently, you are likely to repeat the same mistake again. Sometimes the process of forgiveness can lead to learning naturally, but it is no guarantee, so forgiveness is the middle of the A-Loop and your road to becoming indispensable. While you might feel better at this juncture, the journey isn't over and you must keep moving to the next step along the A-Loop to achieve the level of success you desire.

Now it's time to rectify any areas of your life where judgment against yourself or others is stopping you from making progress on your dreams and Picture of Success. After you complete the exercise below, read on to see how to optimize learning so that you are well positioned to achieve success.

Exercise: Using the Pain of Your Past as a Stepping Stone for Future Success

Think back on your past and identify any feelings of tightness due to guilt, resentment, disappointment, anger, or upset, whether they are in relation to your boss, your family, yourself, or even the government. Remember that whatever negativity you are feeling is stuck inside of you and has little or no direct impact on the source of that tension. It is for you to clear. Now choose one or more of these tools to clear that upset from inside of you:

Option 1: Use the process of self-forgiveness.

Option 2: Do free-form writing.

Option 3: Hold someone accountable in a supportive manner

In particular, notice how you feel afterward—the feeling of freedom, the clarity you have for problem solving and the peace you experience that strengthens you to pursue your life dreams and career Picture of Success.

CHAPTER 8:
SELF-EXAMINATION TO FOSTER SOLUTIONS

Self-Examination to Foster Solutions *is the turning point along the A-Loop. After determining your intention and developing your Picture of Success, you recognized your current reality, determining the gap between your current state and your desired Picture of Success. You were cautioned to not examine for root causes or solutions, because it was too early in the process of being accountable. The reason was simple. Without taking ownership and applying forgiveness, examination can easily be biased—against yourself or others. In addition, examination can easily tend to focus on the past rather than on an exploration of what you can do differently in the future. Self-examination to foster solutions is*

*focused on what you can do differently to be more effective, even
if that means changing something external to you. Ultimately,
personal accountability is about growing, becoming stronger,
and being more successful in how you deal with your external
environment. Self-examination to foster solution is the step along
the A-Loop where you discover how to leverage yourself in resolving old issues and achieving a new level of success.*

> "Problems cannot be solved at the same level of
> awareness that created them."
>
> —Albert Einstein

You have defined success and prioritized the areas that stand
in your way. You have taken ownership for moving forward
and forgiven yourself and others involved. You are perfectly
positioned to begin examining yourself fully and uncovering the
many possible solutions for old issues that have been obstacles to
your success. Self-examination can be one of the most fun stages
of accountability. It's an exploration of options without restric-
tion. During this stage you don't need to make any major decisions. This is when you can be as creative and innovative as you
would like. You aren't bound by old mind-sets, beliefs, behaviors,
actions, or anything else. This is where you get to be the "scientist" in service of generating alternatives.

During this chapter you will learn the art of asking questions
in a way that stimulates your creativity, innovation, and practicality. You will learn how to strengthen and apply critical thinking,
a necessary skill for solving complex problems and taking full
advantage of opportunities. By the time you complete this chapter,
you will be ready to take on meaningful change, achieve better
results, and break through old paradigms.

THE "JUMPING TO SOLUTIONS" TRAP

When we are impatient or pressured by external forces, we can
jump to solutions too quickly. How do you know what is "too

quickly"? Either your solution creates new problems or your solution is a temporary fix that allows the problem to resurface weeks or months later. The purpose of self-examination is to look at problems and challenges differently—from the inside out. Self-examination from the inside out means that instead of fixing something outside of you, you begin by examining your mind-set, behaviors, or emotional responses that either created or are contributing to the problem or challenge. Ultimately, this is the only way to create solutions that are sustainable. Why? Because if your mind-set, behavior, or emotional responses contribute to a breakdown, but you only address the external factors involved in the breakdown, you will re-create that same breakdown over and over. You may have seen this through the many "flavor of the month" change efforts that organizations experience or the never-ending attempt to stay organized at your workstation.

Self-examination is looking at the history, conditions, changes, and patterns that caused the problem to exist in the first place. After exploring the human factors of beliefs, emotions, and behaviors that feed the problem, you can look at the history, conditions, changes, and patterns that are also contributors. It's your discovery in this accountable step that enables you to identify alternative solutions—real solutions that fix the problem for good.

THE IMPORTANCE OF ASKING QUESTIONS

Asking a question opens a door to new solutions for old problems. A question allows you to tap into your creativity. It stimulates your intuition. It gives you access to higher wisdom. It prepares you to be surprised by an original idea. It is the soil of invention, innovation, and discovery.

In contrast, if you *stop* asking questions, you shut doors. You can get stuck in your old ways, beliefs, and attitudes. You draw incorrect conclusions. You make wrong assumptions. Or you feel trapped because you don't see a way out. You think you know it all, and that shuts down your ability to receive information from your inner voice, others, or the universe.

A few years ago, my twelve-year-old daughter came home from school and asked for help on a writing assignment. My first reaction came from the mind-set that I am a poor writer and couldn't help her. That self-judgment shut the door on any possible solution. My second reaction was a judgment of her: "Earlier you wasted time talking on the phone and watching TV. Now it's too late." This was another closed door. My daughter was stuck with her unsolved writing problem, and I was stuck with my frustration.

Then I remembered what I teach: *Ask questions.* Had she been on the phone simply to chat, or had she been trying to get help from her friend? Am I really a poor writer? Do I ever avoid a difficult assignment by crashing in front of the TV? These questions fostered my compassion, understanding, and intuition. This opened up a creative flow. I was able to reconnect with my daughter and help her complete her homework.

A NARROW VIEW OF ACCOUNTABILITY LIMITS SELF-EXAMINATION

A narrow view of accountability can result in narrow involvement during self-examination. For instance, if there is a problem or breakdown and you don't see yourself as part of the problem, you may not participate in the self-examination necessary to solve the problem. But maybe you are more involved than you think.

Many of us were conditioned to think that we are only accountable if we created the problem. When we were younger, we may have heard from our parents, "Your room is a mess. It's your mess; you clean it up!" "Your grades are slipping. They're your grades; you do something about them." Accountability was about cause and effect. If you created a problem, you needed to fix it.

Unfortunately, many people extended that line of thought to "If I didn't cause the problem, it is not my problem." But as I suggested in previous chapters, your accountability doesn't start and stop with what you created. It also includes problems that you are promoting and problems that you are allowing. Let's explore this in more detail.

Whenever there is a breakdown or problem, the most effective way to begin self-examination is to ask, "How am I creating, promoting, or allowing this problem to continue?" We almost always play a role in solving a problem that we aren't directly involved in

---

Exercise: Using Questions to Get Unstuck

Take some time to think of a situation in which you felt stuck. Maybe it was at work, when you were dealing with your boss or a client. Or it might have been at home, when you were dealing with a spouse, a child, or a neighbor. Or it might pertain to travel plans or car problems. Ask yourself the following series of questions to see if the situation could have led to a different outcome:

- Am I making an *assumption* about this situation?

- What *judgments* am I placing against others or myself?

- Do I know anyone who has *dealt successfully* with a similar situation?

- What is the very first thing I can do to make some movement *right now*?

- What *strength* do I have that can assist me in resolving this issue?

- What is *a different way* I could be thinking about this?

Please join the Making Yourself Indispensable community we mentioned in chapter 1 by going to our Web site, www .MarkSamuel.com.

by answering the question, "Is there a way in which I am allowing it to continue?" If there were any question about your role in the problem, asking these questions will quickly surface it and point you in the direction of additional questions.

THE IMPORTANCE OF CRITICAL THINKING
TO SELF-EXAMINATION

To effectively carry out the accountable step of self-examination to foster solutions, you have to combine analysis, intuition, innovation, creativity, and patterning. All of these are what I refer to as critical thinking—the art and skill of looking at a problem or situation from several vantage points. Critical thinking is not about deriving solutions but about asking questions that will lead to alternative solutions. In fact, it is the questions you ask that determine the solutions you get. Unfortunately, people's approach to asking questions can reflect a lack of complete critical thinking. In other words, they head down a trail of one type of question and leave out the many other questions that could be asked to foster a more complete set of possible solutions.

Objectivity

Objectivity is the ability to be *unbiased* and *open* to all other ideas about a problem and its solution. You don't necessarily have to agree with every viewpoint, but you can accept that there are other viewpoints without dismissing them because you disagree. Objectivity is critical for being open to different personalities, communication styles, perspectives, perceptions of the problem, and solutions.

Global View

Global view is the ability to see the "big picture" surrounding a problem or situation. Global view is about seeing the whole or the long-term impact associated with a problem or situation. When global view is in operation, you may not see all of the details, but you will have a sense of the size and shape of the problem. It

would be similar to what you would see if you were in space looking down at earth. You could see the sphere, the size of earth as a
whole, and bodies of water and land. However, you wouldn't see
the borders that separate countries. In business, global view involves
the ability to understand the entire business model and operations
for the organization as well as a long-term strategy for the organization's success in the next five to ten years.

Detail

Detail is the ability to see all the *fine* and *minute* aspects of a problem or situation. It is the opposite of global view in that you are
concerned not with viewing the whole situation but with considering each little detail that is part of the problem—each connection,
each boundary, and the specifics involved. Detail is what you will
want to review before signing a contract, implementing a blue-
print to construct a building or house, or following safety procedures at work.

Perspective

Perspective is the ability to see a situation from *different points of
view.* While objectivity is openness to other points of view, perspective is the ability to put yourself in someone else's shoes to view
the problem through their eyes, beliefs, concerns, and biases. It's
looking at a problem and being able to determine how a woman
might view that problem, how a man might view the problem differently, how a child would view the problem, and how someone
from a different country, religion, economic status, or race might
view the situation. It involves a high level of sensitivity to diverse
thoughts, beliefs, circumstances, and backgrounds.

Symptom-Source Link

Symptom-source link is the ability to *discern the difference between symptoms and root causes* of a problem or situation. It is
the most analytical approach to critical thinking and enables you
to avoid being fooled into solving symptoms and never addressing

the real problem. If you put ointment on a skin rash when the rash is caused by a food allergy, you aren't dealing with the real problem—the source—and are only addressing the symptom. It is essential to differentiate sources from symptoms in order to prevent wasting a lot of time implementing solutions with little or no effect.

Integration

Integration is the ability to *balance and connect all critical-thinking approaches* in order to derive the optimal solutions to a problem. Integration allows you to not overemphasize one or two critical-thinking approaches while ignoring others. It also enables you to see the interconnectedness of the various critical-thinking approaches and the answers you surface. It's through integration that you maintain a healthy balance between a global, long-term perspective and the details of a solution for implementation.

BECOMING A TOP-NOTCH PROBLEM SOLVER THROUGH CRITICAL THINKING

There are four essential principles of critical thinking necessary to optimize your ability to ask questions and solve problems. First, you must apply a balance of critical-thinking abilities. This means that you ask questions about the problem that represent all six critical-thinking abilities. Second, no matter how developed a thinker you are, you will tend to have three areas of critical thinking that represent your natural core strengths and three critical-thinking areas that represent your weaker abilities. You will have a chance to explore this when you complete the exercise at the end of this section. It's very similar to being left-handed or right-handed—you will tend to use one hand more than the other for writing, eating, lifting, etc. The problem here is that if you are using only your critical-thinking strengths to determine the questions you ask, you will inadvertently leave out questions that would lead you to a more effective solution. Third, your critical-thinking strength becomes a weakness when it is overused. In other words, if your critical-thinking strength is *detail* and you get too detailed in your questioning, the discussion of the potential solutions gets sidetracked by the many detailed questions that get surfaced. Fourth, you can improve upon your critical-thinking weak areas through specific skill-building training or by extending your problem-solving efforts to include others with different critical-thinking strengths. The challenge of including others is that your ego wants to solve the problem itself. Also, if you are open to including others, it's more comfortable and validating to include others who think like you. Sometimes you may even reject others who think differently. But without ego issues getting in the way, organizations have a natural and effective way to increase critical thinking: the use of cross-functional engagement.

THE VALUE OF CROSS-FUNCTIONAL PROBLEM SOLVING

Being indispensable doesn't mean that you are solving every problem by yourself. In fact, that is a good way to become dispensable very quickly. The more indispensable you are, the more you include others in your problem-solving process. You are smart enough to realize that the ability to solve problems depends not on how smart you are but on how many different critical-thinking attributes you are using to solve a problem. And this requires involving others in your process.

One other discovery we made in the process of studying critical thinking is that each functional area generally has similar dominating critical-thinking abilities that support the people in that function to effectively do their jobs. For instance, it is very common for people working in human resources to have a strong ability in *perspective*. They can take almost any problem and know how individual contributors, people on the line, the customer, and people in top management would view and react to that problem. While this is a strength, it can turn into a weakness if they can't make a decision due to concern about how a particular group will respond. Engineers are typically strong in *detail* and *symptom-source link*. Their conversations could easily get sidetracked by the details of a project and the never-ending quest to find the single root cause while losing sight of the outcomes they are trying to accomplish.

By getting people from different functional areas together to solve a problem, you will be including different critical-thinking strengths and ensuring that you are asking as many different kinds of questions as are necessary to effectively solve a problem. This is a great value that middle managers can create by getting together to solve problems, even if some problems stem from just one functional area.

I worked with an operations management team that comprised three different functional areas. The three functional managers within operations were in complete conflict and polarization. You couldn't get them in a room together to solve a common problem, since it always resulted in a blame game and attacks against one another, which put them fully into the Victim Loop. When I talked to them about the six critical-thinking approaches and the need to use all six to solve a problem, it made sense to them. And when I brought up the idea that the three of them had different critical-thinking approaches that were being negated by one another, they also agreed with that assessment. In fact, one of the team members claimed, "In reviewing the most recent conflicts we had, it stemmed from making each other wrong for how we were thinking about a particular problem. In fact, I thought that another way to look at the problem was stupid, because I couldn't see it from their perspective." They looked at one another, smiled, and nodded in agreement that they had all had the same reaction to one another. With this realization, they decided to value one another's different thinking approaches and established a process of team problem solving to take advantage of their differences. Their "conflict" was immediately resolved, and we didn't need to apply any conflict-resolution techniques or negotiation strategies.

We simply raised their awareness of diverse thinking and taught them to value one another rather than dismissing one another.

Chris, the plant manager whose team was constantly late in meeting its deliverables, applied this critical-thinking concept in his meetings. Before getting coached, he was the one driving all of the solutions. He was smarter, more experienced, and more competent than others on the team but had little to do with finding optimal solutions, especially when things needed to be done differently from before. With coaching, he involved his team in solving problems and began using the different critical-thinking abilities of his cross-functional management team. In this way he was able to surface brand-new solutions to old problems. Besides generating more ownership from his team, he also developed diverse thinking that helped everyone on the team to think in ways different from

Exercise: Improve Your Critical Thinking

1. Based on your self-assessment, which of the following critical-thinking abilities represent your strengths and which your areas of relative weakness? (Circle the one that applies.)

    Objectivity: Strength or Weakness
    Global view: Strength or Weakness
    Detail: Strength or Weakness
    Perspective: Strength or Weakness
    Symptom-source link: Strength or Weakness
    Integration: Strength or Weakness

2. Whom do you know who has different critical-thinking abilities that you could begin to include in your problem-solving efforts?

their comfort zone. For the first time they were coming up with new approaches to improve efficiency and effectiveness.

DIGGING DEEPER FOR ANSWERS

Because actions produce results, when we don't like our results we first look to change our actions. But in many cases our actions are symptoms of our thinking and our emotions. In one example, George, a supervisor, requested input from his direct reports during team meetings, in accordance with the organization's desire for greater employee engagement. He was frustrated that his direct reports never spoke up. Assuming that they had nothing to say, he had stopped asking for their input. Upon further exploration, I discovered that George felt he should be able to lead his group without their input. After all, he was the boss. So several months earlier, when he had asked for input, he had rejected their ideas without consideration. His team had learned to not bother participating. To solve this problem, it was necessary to reframe George's beliefs about being a supervisor, his need for control, and his skill in dealing with conflicting ideas without resulting in conflict. It was George's self-examination that uncovered the root causes of the problem, which no amount of behavior changing could have addressed. Digging deeper means looking past the actions to the mind-set and emotions that could be a root cause of the problem.

Let's look at each of the factors that allow you to dig deeper in more detail.

Belief

A belief is a mental state made up of our mind-set, assumptions, and convictions. It influences our attitude, behavior, and choices. Walt Disney once said, "If you can dream it, you can do it." That belief manifested a radical transformation in the way people experienced entertainment and fun. Similarly, the operations management team discussed earlier first needed to see themselves as a team and commit to being one, not just getting along but being interdependent. They couldn't succeed without the support of one another.

Emotions

Emotions are the feelings that trigger our reactions. Charles Schwab said, "A man can succeed at almost anything for which he has unlimited enthusiasm." Emotions are the engine behind the self-confidence and trust you need to get up and go.

The opposite is also true. If you approach them with discouragement and doubt, you can fail at the simplest tasks. The operations management team had emotional distress because they avoided dealing with their unresolved conflict. They needed a structure to address conflicts. It wasn't enough to just be sensitive and understanding of their differences. They needed to create a *process* to resolve conflict.

Behaviors

Behaviors are the way we conduct ourselves and the actions that produce results. Benjamin Disraeli said, "Action may not always bring happiness, but there is no happiness without action." Ultimately, it's the improvement of your *behavior* that enables you to reach excellence. The operations management team created common practices for developing teamwork and accomplishing their initiatives.

You may have heard that the definition of insanity is doing the same thing over and over expecting a different result. Well, the same holds true with your thoughts, feelings, and beliefs. If you keep repeating the same thoughts that trigger the same feelings and keep functioning from the same set of beliefs that got you where you are, you are going to keep creating the same reality around you. It's critical to ask questions and examine the relationship among your mind-set, emotions, and behavior.

SELF-EXAMINATION IS A LINCHPIN
OF INDISPENSABILITY

While self-examination is one of the steps in the A-Loop, high achievers and those who are indispensable do not use it only in the order of the loop. When you are indispensable, you are always looking for opportunities to improve and evolve to higher levels of excellence. This means you are in the "game" of asking questions: How do I improve my communication, my efficiency, my quality, my customer service, and my teamwork? The subject matter is endless and the questions are constant. These people aren't waiting for something to break to go through the process of self-

Exercise: Exploring "Automatic Pilot" Responses

Find a friend to ask you the following questions. The only rule is that he or she can't give you any advice or pass any judgment. However, your friend can repeat a question if he or she feels you can go deeper in your response. The goal is to go as deep as you can and get the most out of this exercise.

1. What is one aspect of your performance, communication, behavior, or attitude that you would like to improve?

2. When does it show up as a problem in your life?

3. How do you create, promote, or allow this problem to continue?

4. How does it benefit you to *not* improve this issue?

5. What does it *cost* you to not improve this issue?

6. What could you do differently to be more effective?

7. What support would you like from others?

8. What is the next small action you can take, and when will you take it?

9. What will it look, sound, and feel like when you are more successful?

examination to foster solutions. They are always open to asking questions that challenge current ways of functioning, even when those ways worked well in the past. Those who are indispensable know that a good solution that solved a past problem may result in current breakdowns or be an obstacle to a future Picture of Success.

You can avoid a lot of grief or shorten the time you are stuck in frustration, disappointment, or discouragement by using self-examination to ask yourself questions that will lead to new perspectives, new approaches, new thinking, and ultimately a different way to do things to get better results.

It is very exciting to have fresh ideas, new responses, and alternative solutions for moving forward on your Picture of Success. *Self-examination to foster solutions* puts you in the driver's seat for learning, making decisions, and eventually taking action to make a difference. But don't get ahead of yourself. Make sure you are mastering the learning process that is represented in the next step along the A-Loop. While previous steps were partly focused on avoiding the move down into the Victim Loop, the next step to become a Master Learner is used for optimizing the solutions you have developed to attain your Picture of Success. You are close now, so keep moving on the A-Loop to become indispensable.

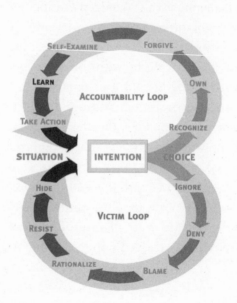

After completing the accountable step of self-examination to foster solutions, you must become a Master Learner to sort out the alternatives and decide on your next actions. In fact, self-examination and being a Master Learner go hand in hand. Becoming a Master Learner is about seizing the opportunity to let yourself be transformed. Think differently. Integrate a new behavior that serves your purpose—to actualize your Picture of Success. You dealt with the past through the steps on the A-Loop of recognizing your current reality, taking ownership, and applying forgiveness. Now you are in the middle of the three steps that

are moving you directly toward your Picture of Success and indis-
pensability.

> "The illiterate of the 21st century will not be those
> who cannot read or write, but those who cannot
> learn, unlearn and relearn."
>
> —Alvin Toffler

Self-examination is the appetizer, while learning is the main course. Learning is the most important competency for anyone wanting to be indispensable—learning new skills, learning new habits, learning to correct a mistake, and learning to improve performance. No matter what you are learning, it is the basis for change, for improvement, and for success—lasting success. The day you stop learning is the day you become dispensable—stuck in your old way of doing things, stuck in your old responses, stuck in your dysfunctional attitude, behavior, and actions. While self-examination opens new doors, learning is walking through the door to a new level of success, a new life.

You can use your own style of learning. Some have to "see" it to understand it. Some need to "hear" it to make it ring true for them. Others need to "feel" it to get the full sense of the change. But regardless of your style and approach to learning, do it! Dedicate yourself to learning something new each and every day. The Master Learner is a student of life. This doesn't mean you attend college forever without graduating. The Master Learner is a student of effectiveness, efficiency, and improvement that is based on practical application in his or her world at work and at home. One of my first business partners, Tom, was the first person I met who had a systematic approach to learning. While working for a major multinational petroleum company, he had been promoted eight times in eleven years and was now working for the CEO. When asked about one of his secrets to success, he responded by talking about his "learning journal." He would keep a journal by his bedside. Before going to bed, he would write down what he had learned that day. He had years of learning that he recorded and reviewed periodically. Tom was a Master Learner.

THE BIGGEST BARRIER TO BECOMING
A MASTER LEARNER

In general there are two kinds of learning situations. One kind of learning is being presented new information, a new skill, or a new awareness that you were never exposed to in the past. Except for the fear you might have about integrating something new that you aren't used to, there is little emotional disturbance associated with this kind of learning situation. But this kind of learning situation alone won't make you a Master Learner. We have all met people who were book smart but couldn't get along in the world. They lacked experience in the second kind of learning situation—the school of hard knocks.

The school of hard knocks represents the other kind of situation we learn from—mistakes of all shapes and sizes. The challenge all of us have with the "school of hard knocks" approach to learning is that before we get to the learning we have to deal with the judgments, disappointments, rejection, and punishment that many times accompany mistakes. Whether these come from our boss, our teammates, our spouse, our parents, or even ourselves, it hurts to let others down, and they may add to our pain by their judgment and criticism. If we get caught in the emotional and sometimes physical pain associated with mistakes, we may never get to the learning. Even worse, we may avoid the natural risks of life that are necessary in order to improve our situation, such as developing new or more intimate relationships, taking steps to improve our career, or addressing breakdowns in our performance or communication.

This is a core obstacle to becoming a Master Learner—we are so afraid of the consequences of making mistakes that we play it safe, don't try new approaches, don't challenge methods that don't work, and keep ourselves from taking risks that could result in a breakdown. Of course, the result of avoiding negative consequences is that you stop learning and remain stuck at whatever level of functioning you currently hold while people around you are continuing to improve. The outcome: a fast track to dispensability.

Master Learners know that they must learn from mistakes instead of deflecting them, blaming others for them, or hiding from them, which leads right back into the Victim Loop. They have had to develop the courage to change the consequences game from one of punishment to one of learning—every time, no matter what. And if they get punished by others, they still have a default response of learning from the experience rather than giving up in defeat. For an indispensable person who has made a mistake and suffered a punishing consequence, winning means learning from the mistake.

Once you have the commitment and courage to be a Master Learner, you are ready to adopt three basic steps to enhance your learning experience.

THREE EASY STEPS TO LEARNING

The first step is becoming *aware* of what works and what doesn't work about your role in the problem area that has surfaced. If you aren't aware of what takes you off track, it will be hard for you to correct it the next time it shows up. This could be as simple as the awareness that you are getting defensive or anxious, which causes you to communicate in a less effective manner, or the awareness that when your boss is talking to you, you get tongue-tied or say things to sabotage your strength. One middle manager I coached had a pattern of overcommunicating in meetings with his peers. Even though he had good points to make, others would roll their eyes whenever he spoke. He couldn't change this reaction until he saw the pattern. Initially he blamed others for their reaction to him, which is why the second step to learning is critical.

The second step to effective learning is *understanding*. Do you understand what is behind your behavior, reaction, or attitude? Through the step of understanding, the middle manager discovered that he wanted approval and to be respected by his peers. He would overcommunicate to make sure he was heard, but it had the opposite effect. His good thinking would get lost in the overcommunication, and his peers would dismiss him. Gaining that understanding was critical to his learning a new approach but had to be followed up by the third step before he could act differently.

The third step to learning is *motivation*. What is motivating you to make the change? Maybe you are internally motivated by your desire for a different result, or maybe you are motivated by external drivers. External motivators could be the fear of losing your job, preventing a punishment-oriented consequence like a traffic ticket, or being embarrassed one more time in front of your peers. The middle manager wanted to become a more effective leader with greater influence, so he was very interested in identifying ways in which he undermined himself and learning new approaches to use his good critical-thinking skills to improve team effectiveness. He was internally motivated.

CURIOSITY—THE MASTER LEARNER COMPETENCY

The foundation for any Master Learner is curiosity. A Master Learner will ask questions like "What might it look like to improve beyond current standards of excellence?" "How can we communicate with greater understanding through our differences?" and "What can I do to contribute more to the team?" Whether your curiosity is about taking care of equipment, improving performance, or developing more intimate relationships, it drives you to find ways to change, adjust, and rise to a new standard of excellence. Curiosity allows you to explore and try new things just to find out if you can stumble across a process, method, or approach that not only breaks the norm but also discovers a creative way to achieve better results.

IS YOUR CURIOSITY SERVING YOU?

While our focus on learning and curiosity has been positive, it is important to look at the dark side of those wonderful attributes.

Is your curiosity leading you to your Picture of Success? If you are so curious about the taste of the delicious-looking dessert that you devour it, your curiosity just sabotaged your goal of losing weight. If you are curious whether anyone at work will notice that you are taking longer breaks or not picking up the phone when a customer calls, you are not leading yourself to excellence. It is important to keep your curiosity pointed toward your vision and picture of excellence. It's never about curiosity for the sake of curiosity—that can get you in real trouble. It's curiosity that starts alcohol and drug addictions. It's curiosity that makes you think you can get away with less than your best at work. Make sure your curiosity is working for you, serving you, and leading to betterment. Keep your curiosity focused on your desired Picture of Success.

TRAPS THAT PREVENT LEARNING

We say we want to learn, but do we really? I often encounter people who seem committed to their growth but get caught in their own stumbling blocks—their emotions, mind-set, or behavioral habits. They go to workshops, read books and gain advice from others but they don't seem to change their work habits, communication or life for the better. Sometimes, their ego position of know-it-all or their lack of self-esteem gets in the way.

I coached Virginia who always said, "I get it. I understand." In her case, she didn't. She was so ashamed of acknowledging she didn't understand something that she had developed the reflex of saying "I understand" when she really didn't. This made learning impossible. To learn, you need the openness and the courage to know that you do not know everything. This leads us to the first of seven traps that prevent true learning.

Trap #1: "I can do this myself."

Whether it is to prove their value to their organization, demonstrate how smart they are, or simply maintain control, there are some people who pretend to know what they don't know. They spout made-up facts to demonstrate their knowledge in a discussion, or they lead projects themselves without bringing in the employees or consultants who have the experience to be successful. They want the credit and need to feel in control—no matter what. I coached Cindy, who was leading the effort to shut down and reopen a plant while equipment and technology were being upgraded. She had been a very competent leader in her old role, but this was a development opportunity for her. Her previous success had been a result of working superhard, being a fast learner, and taking control of details. However, in this new project-leadership role she didn't have the technical expertise or the project management experience to manage by herself. Cindy's boss and mentor offered to hire a project manager who was an expert in shutdowns, but she refused the help, saying, "I can handle this myself." She was coached by her boss to accept the role of project facilitator and to use the necessary experts to support her effort. However, she had too great a need to control to understand her boss's logic. After three months of missing target dates, Cindy found herself so far behind that she was removed from the position and reassigned. Cindy needed to do it herself and stay in control, which kept her from learning. Without learning there was no change in her performance or results.

Trap #2: "It's not the way we do things around here. We are unique."

There is comfort in the familiar. People caught in this trap cling to their current reality and feel threatened by new approaches. Sometimes it's the fear of failure, but many times it's simply "I don't want to make the effort to learn something new."

Recently a small printing company hired me to help its production manager to optimize his space in preparation for the growth of the company. I was struck by the manager's habits. He was *proud* to tell me how the place had not changed in the last three years. He had his process down. He did one job at a time. All of the supplies were kept in one part of the large room. But it was clear that if efficiencies were to be improved, he would need to handle multiple jobs at the same time. He would also need to move his supplies closer to the equipment where those supplies were used. Although he was willing to move the supplies, he was not willing to change his process. Within six months, management replaced him with another production manager, who modified the process to handle multiple jobs—and productivity increased by 35 percent. If you have the attitude of "It's not the way we do things around here," you may suddenly find yourself in a position of "I'm not the kind of person they keep around here."

Trap #3: "It wasn't invented here."

This might be an issue of control or ego. I have seen this syndrome in managers who wouldn't accept an idea from their direct reports until it was presented as their own idea. I've also seen parents taking credit for an idea their child came up with. And I've seen organizations that would not accept a tool from a consultant because the organization's full-time staff didn't create that tool.

I recently worked with a senior management team for a clothing retail chain. I had been teaching the principles of accountability to their direct reports (middle managers) for a couple of weeks when senior management began receiving feedback that their direct reports were more focused in team meetings, more open to collaborating cross-functionally, and more effectively prioritizing their projects and tasks. They seemed to respect my approach. Even the skeptics seemed convinced that it was going to bring positive change.

Given that success, I invited them to use a project-management form that I had developed over the previous twenty years. That they refused. They wanted to make up their own form. One of their assistants kept me informed that they implemented five different management forms in three months, but none worked for them. They were stuck.

When you have to invent everything yourself, you are apt to learn from trial and error, which is the slowest way to learn. It is important to learn from others who have come before you and have the experience to know how to avoid common mistakes. This speeds up learning even though you may pay for the education.

Trap #4: "Prove it to me."

Some people can't try anything new, or even accept the validity of a new approach if it can't be proved.

Matt, the manager of educational services at a major teaching hospital in Houston, asked me to make a presentation to John, his director of organizational development. Matt had experienced major improvements in his previous hospital when I worked with managers to improve cross-functional teamwork. He was convinced that I could address the territorialism that existed within his new organization.

When I presented our methodology to John, it was clear that he was skeptical. He immediately asked for proof that our team system and accountability technology worked. I shared with him the results of several health-care organizations, including some that were teaching hospitals. Matt shared his experience in the meeting as well. But John was still resistant. He said, "No, I want to understand the *theories* that are the basis of your work." I told him the basis of my work involved an integration of many theories of leadership, including those of Abraham Maslow, Edward Lawler, Newton Margulies, Kenneth Blanchard, and Kurt Lewin. However, the methodology truly comes from my being a practitioner. John was not impressed, and my client references and previous history of measurable results made no difference. There was nothing I could have done to prove it to him. He decided to search for a proven solution based on the theories he had learned in college. When I checked in with him a year later, he still hadn't brought in a consultant to achieve his goals. Nothing ever changed in his organization.

Proof is helpful, but it's not the only way to make decisions. Experience and intuition are essential components.

TEACHERS AND STUDENTS

We are all teachers and students—it happens without having the formal role. While my clients hire me as an expert in accountability and making yourself indispensable, my view is that I am a *student* of accountability. And I have been a student of accountability for over twenty-five years. It is being a student that has caused others to consider me an expert. And at the moment I stop learning more about accountability, I will be giving up my status as an expert. There is always more to learn.

Learning is the outcome of every relationship we are in and every action we take. It begins in the relationship between parents and children. While we think it is the parents who set up the rules, children come in with their own personalities and needs, which teaches their parents how to respond to them. My school buddy Bob was one of the most studious people I knew growing up. He got straight *A*s, won academic awards in high school, and eventually graduated with honors from Stanford University. At the same time, Bob did very poorly in sports. He always had difficulty in gym class and never did well in after-school sports. It just wasn't his strength. As a result, he lacked not only any interest in playing sports but also any interest in being a spectator. He didn't go to the games and never really learned about the different sports. Bob married Alice, who was also very bright and not very athletic and had no interest in sports. However, when they had their second son, Tom, their lives changed forever. Tom was totally into sports. He had strong skills in basketball and soccer. Being supportive parents, Bob and Alice helped their son develop his athletic interests. As a result, they not only learned to play each of those sports but also learned to enjoy those sports as spectators.

In relationships we are constantly learning and teaching each other. If one person in the relationship tends to take on the role of accommodator, then the other person in the relationship *learns* to take the lead in making decisions and taking initiative. This can eventually be detrimental to the relationship when the dynamics change. For instance, George was the accommodator in his relationship with his wife. He loved to please his wife and accommodated her needs—gladly. However, over time George began to feel like his needs weren't getting met, and he became resentful that his wife was always making the decisions for the family. He didn't remember that he had *taught* his wife to make decisions by playing the passive role of an accommodator.

The same is true at work. I've seen managers who want to be respected and in control of the teams they manage. They insist on making the decisions when there is a problem. They create an environment where their direct reports come to them when they have a conflict or when they have a problem that needs solving. In the case of one manager I worked with, at first this served him in developing his self-confidence. However, as the organization grew and resources became limited, he didn't have time to make every decision and solve every problem. He had to rely on his direct reports to step up in their leadership. By this time it was too late. His direct reports didn't have the thinking skills or the habits to solve problems among themselves. Their manager had *taught* them to be dependent on him.

Because we are all teachers and students of one another, it is important that we take responsibility for what we are learning from others and teaching those close to us. We must become aware of the impact we have on others as well as the impact others have on us to determine if adjustments need to be made in our relationships—whether at work or at home.

> The first problem for all of us, men and women, is not to learn, but to unlearn.
>
> —Gloria Steinem

LET THE LEARNING COME FROM INSIDE OF YOU

Master Learners don't learn only from external sources like books, experts, and people on their team. While it is not taught in most schools or universities, I have met many high performers and

Exercise: Exploring Your Teacher and Learner Relationships

Identify two or three of your most important relationships at work and at home and answer the following questions for each relationship.

1. What are you teaching each of those people by your attitude, behavior, and actions?

2. Is what you are teaching them serving you and the relationship? How?

3. What can you do differently to teach them differently through your attitude, behavior, and actions that would benefit you and/or the relationship?

4. What are the costs of not making the change?

5. What is your first step in making the change?

6. What are you learning from each of those relationships?

7. Is what you are learning serving you and the relationship?

8. What could you do differently to change your learning relationship in order to more effectively support yourself and the relationship?

9. What is your first step in making the change?

indispensable people who have developed the ability to "listen" within themselves for answers to questions. This is an important skill and ability to develop, which I was first introduced to when I was thirty. Today it is one of my most important methods for learning.

There is an incredible wisdom within us that we tend to forget because we are so accustomed to looking for answers outside ourselves—from the Internet, television, training, books by experts, and now Twitter. These sources bombard us with information, so much so that our inner voice can get a little lost in all the chaos. It is an important muscle to develop—listening to the inner voice inside of us. And there are some keys for effective *inner listening*.

The first key is to have a clear internal intention. The "voice" will respond more when we have a positive and clear direction than when we are in a state of fear. This isn't because the voice does anything differently. It is just that when we are in a state of fear, we aren't listening. Instead we are running our negative scenarios, so there is no room for listening. As we think of our Picture of Success or our intention, we can put our mind in a state of calm.

The second key is to ask a clear question that is directional in nature and to which you would like to hear an answer from inside you. It could be a question like "What is the best way for me to prepare for the meeting I have with my boss?" or "What is an approach to solving the conflict I have with my teammate?" It could even be "What advice do 'you' have for me in moving forward on my desire to improve my performance?"

The third key is to patiently wait for an answer in silence. Sometimes it can take a while, and it is important that you aren't in an active mode to find an answer. Let it come to you. And if you get distracted by other thoughts entering your mind, just acknowledge them and let them go. Don't try to prevent them or do anything with them. Keep returning to your listening. Also, you can do things to disengage your mind, which is usually the block to listening. This could include taking a walk, playing a round of golf, or listening to music or taking a nap. Some people meditate or do yoga to nurture this process. Most important, there is no right way to do this. You need to experiment to find your best way to listen internally.

The fourth key is to listen for any message at all, and if it doesn't make sense, ask the voice to give you more information about the message. Sometimes you can literally start a conversation with the voice, and it can be quite profound.

The final key is to take action on what you hear. This doesn't mean to jump into the answer with both feet, because that may be too risky. Test the answer you are receiving by taking small steps if you can, or by talking to others you trust who have wisdom in the area of your question before making a major decision that has significant consequences. It's similar to entering a pool of water the temperature of which you don't know. You first put your toes in the water . . . then your ankles, and so on until your entire body is immersed. You always want to be the scientist, checking out the validity of any voice giving you advice—whether it is someone else or your inner voice.

As you develop your inner voice, you will begin to get many messages during the day. And as your inner voice gets stronger and stronger, you will find that it sometimes sounds different. Sometimes it appears to be more emotionally based, while other times it is more pure, as if it comes from a neutral, *higher* part of you. And beyond these two distinctions, you might discern different "parts" of you that are getting your attention. While the "higher self" voice is the most pure and one to act on, the others could be either positive or negative. Therefore, with all other voices you must be discerning. I am discerning with all voices I hear so that I get better at being able to differentiate the "higher self" voice from the others.

- The *critic* is demanding. He teaches you to never quit, to expect a lot of yourself, and to deliver impeccable work.

- The *higher self* connects you to the universe. He teaches you to trust what is to come and who is to come in support of your intention and Picture of Success.

- The *rebel* reminds you to question what's established. He teaches you to challenge rules that might not work

anymore, especially when it comes to outdated procedures and processes.

- The *creative* inspires you to look for different solutions, to look upside down and inside out, just to see if
there is another way, which is critical for effective
problem solving.

- The *scared* protects you. He is the one who will remind
you to wear safety gear, to "look both ways" when
crossing the street or implementing a new process at
work.

- The *inner child* pouts, whines, and reminds you to
take a nap or go play when you have been overworking.

- The *competitor* is in the game of winning and supports you in driving to be the best. He's the one who
wants to feel valued, worthy, and in control.

It is important to know which of these parts is being activated
within you—to learn how to listen to yourself with discerning
ears—in order to respond accordingly. Maybe what you're hearing is a call to take action to improve your performance or to slow
down in order to improve the quality of your work, or maybe it
is a signal that you are too tired to push for another hour on a
project. These parts provide great assistance in learning how to
respond to different situations so as to be more successful.

Being a Master Learner is also staying aware of whom you are
bringing to the table when meeting with others. Are you bringing
your *competitor*, who is causing you difficult relationships with
others? Are you bringing your *rebel*, who is resisting change? Are
you choosing which part of yourself you are bringing to the table,
or is it choosing you based on an old story that is no longer serving you?

Paula, the employee with promise, discovered through an

effective coach that when she was on the job, there was an "insecure little girl" who showed up with her. This part of her was afraid of being found out as a fraud—not as good as her previous employers had thought. As a result, she would undermine herself and then blame others—much as an immature child might—making herself dispensable. This was a defense mechanism to deal with the pressure of performing at a high standard. Once she was aware of that part of her, she could calm that insecure part and give a voice to the competent part of her that could stand the pressure of high performance. This was a key part of her changing her performance on her third hire, opening up her career to move in a positive direction again.

> To know others is wisdom; to know yourself is enlightenment.
>
> —Lao-tzu

TASTING THE FREEDOM OF BECOMING INDISPENSABLE

Now you have traveled through *recognizing* areas for improvement and your unique strengths; taking *ownership* of utilizing your strengths to address weaker areas; *forgiving* yourself and others so that you are making accountable agreements and have effective recovery strategies when things get off track; and *self-examining* to apply your critical thinking to effectively solve the problems and challenges to moving forward; and as a *Master Learner* on the A-Loop you are using every situation as an opportunity for advancement and improvement. You are currently on an upward cycle of growing your awareness, understanding, competency, and emotional intelligence. You are well on your way to indispensability.

People are noticing the difference when you walk into a room with a new level of confidence, participate in meetings, sharing your wisdom and innovative ideas, and surface the problem that everyone else is too embarrassed to talk about. You are demon-strating a higher level of courage, curiosity, compassion, and understanding—the qualities that are beginning to make you of great value to those around you. But you aren't done yet. While

---

Exercise: Integrate Your Discoveries

Part 1: Be the scientist

1. List five different lessons you have learned from reading this book. These can include awareness about yourself and your relationships with others, new strategies for being success-ful, or fresh approaches for making changes in your life.

2. Identify any patterns across your five lessons:

    •   Is there a common theme?

    •   Do they focus on a particular area (mind-set, emotions, behaviors)?

    •   Are there environmental conditions that link to these lessons?

3. What are your conclusions? What actions can you take for improvement?

Part 2: Keep a journal
Take time to list what you have learned at the end of every day. This can be a five-minute or longer exercise that becomes your encyclopedia of personal wisdom. Then, once a month, take time to review what you have written during the month. Notice what has changed in your life and what you still want to improve.

becoming a Master Learner puts you in the game of being indispensable, you must take the next step on the A-Loop, the final step of the process, in order to become indispensable. Move on and take action to make manifest what you have been focusing on from the first step of setting intention and developing your Picture of Success.

CHAPTER 10:
TAKE ACTION TO BE SUCCESSFUL

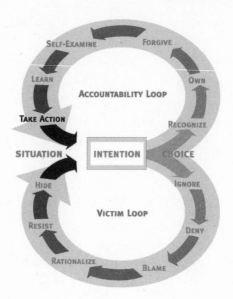

You have done the work of following the A-Loop to bring you to this final step toward becoming indispensable. After clarifying your intention and Picture of Success, you diligently followed the path of accountability to recognize, own, and forgive where you came from, and you engaged in self-examination and learning to identify where you must go next to achieve a new level of success. You are set up for the final step, taking action, to take what you have done and manifest your Picture of Success. To achieve your dreams, goals, and Picture of Success you have to make each action you take important. There is no wrong action as long as it

is consistent with your desired outcomes. You may not achieve success immediately, but each step provides experience and lessons necessary for taking better actions the next time. Are your actions deliberate, random, impulsive, or chaotic? This chapter is about taking small, deliberate steps toward making yourself indispensable and enjoying the success that ensues.

> "Even if you are on the right track, you will get run over if you just sit there."
>
> —Will Rogers

N othing you have read in this book will do you any good if you don't *take action* on what you have learned.

The final and irrevocable reality is this: As important as ownership, self-awareness, and learning are in the achievement of your dreams, they won't get you anywhere in and of themselves. *Action* is essential.

TAKE A STEP, ANY STEP

It doesn't matter if you take a wrong step, but the surest way to fail at reaching your goals is to remain in place. The minute you stop moving, you ruin your chance of reaching your final destination. On the other hand, if you're in motion, whether it is forward, sideways, or even backward, success simply becomes a matter of navigation.

Accountability does not exist without action. Remember the definition: *Accountability is taking action consistent with your desired outcomes.* You can't remove "taking action" from the equation. No action = no accountability. And with no accountability, you will get poor results. Jim Collins discusses the importance of results to Level 5 leaders in his book *Good to Great* when he says, "Level 5 leaders are fanatically driven, infected with an incurable need to produce results." When you are indispensable, you are dedicated to taking action that produces successful results.

TAKING ACTION HAS POWERFUL BENEFITS

The first benefit of taking action occurs *internally*. The more you act, the more you learn about whatever you are doing—what works and doesn't work. Over time you become more effective, more efficient, and more confident that you know what you are doing. You initiate momentum. Movement provides the energy to continue making progress. The hardest thing is getting started, whether it's getting organized at work, starting that new project, or initiating a difficult conversation. But once started, the momentum builds until you reach completion. Between the experiences you gain and the momentum that propels you forward, taking action builds your self-confidence, trust in yourself, and ultimately a sense of freedom.

I coached Dawn, who was the director of operations for an international nonprofit organization. She was a very effective leader and well respected by upper management and her direct reports. She was a great coach and mentor to the people who reported to her. However, Dawn's level of satisfaction and fulfillment from her job was waning. She was getting burned out and her health was declining. She had gained significant weight and was spending more days out sick and seeing a variety of health practitioners. She blamed her job and the changes that the organization was making as the root cause of her unhappiness.

In one of our coaching sessions, Dawn shared her frustration with her job. Using the steps of the A-Loop, I asked what she loved most about her job. She responded without hesitation, "Coaching and mentoring my direct reports. I love to see people grow and be part of their growth." I knew this was part of her intention or Picture of Success. Then I asked Dawn what she did to relieve the pressures of her job. Again she responded without taking a breath, "Art! I love doing art. When I am doing art I am in a complete state of peace and joy—like the rest of the world doesn't exist." It was clear that coaching people and doing art were both part of Dawn's Picture of Success. Moving to the step of self-examination, I asked, "What can you do to combine your love of art with your

love of coaching?" This time Dawn was stumped. Those represented "two different worlds" that she had never thought of com-
bining. I reminded her that we were just brainstorming and there
was no need to have the "solution." Freed from having to be practical, Dawn blurted out unexpectedly her idea of teaching or
coaching people in art as a vehicle for self-development. Even she
was surprised at the words that came out of her mouth.

For the next year, Dawn spent her time making excuses for
not pursuing this idea. She had no experience. She couldn't give up
her job and the steady income. She didn't know anything about
running her own business. All good reasons for not moving forward. But as the year progressed, Dawn gained more weight, her
health continued to decline, and she became increasingly unhappy
with her job.

Having a clear intention or Picture of Success but not acting
upon it is similar to pinching a rubber hose when water is flowing
through it. The pressure builds until it bursts. The pressure on Dawn
was building and needed to be released. The key to taking action
when it seems like a huge mountain to climb is taking one step at
a time. I suggested to Dawn that she didn't need to change her day
job to begin a workshop on weekends or nights. And she didn't
need to be skilled in business, marketing, or sales to get started
either. All she needed to do was to create an artful flyer announc-
ing her new class and ask her friends who wanted to participate.
She didn't even need to charge money except to cover the cost of
materials. Based on this feedback, and with encouragement from
her husband, Dawn sent an e-mail to her friends about starting
a new art workshop for personal growth. She also stocked her
garage with art supplies and cleared a space to start the workshop.

Dawn took the step and, with four of her friends showing up,
started a once-a-week workshop in her garage for eight weeks. At
the end of the workshop, all of her friends asked for four more
weeks and insisted on paying Dawn for her time. They also spread
the word and six people called Dawn to sign up for her next workshop. This one small step to get started led to the next until a year

later she had quit her job and was facilitating three workshops each week with thirty participants. She also had four coaching clients doing art for personal growth. She was in business and doing well. More important, Dawn lost twenty-five pounds and improved her health by being less stressed and doing what she loved doing—art and coaching—and making money doing it.

Once you make the choice and overcome your fear, you develop the confidence to take on bigger challenges. By accepting that you *alone* are accountable for your own success, happiness, and self-fulfillment, you realize that you *alone* can build the courage and the drive to go after what you want to achieve.

Action also builds other people's trust in you. When you take action—even if you don't always fully accomplish your goals—you prove that you're willing to accept challenges and try new things. *You* become the one who *gets things done*. Dawn had built this kind of trust in her old job but took that trust to a new level when she started a business around her core passion in life. Your willingness to act also helps others break through the barriers of fear. Once they see *you* take action, they will find the courage to do the same. Dawn not only assisted people in developing their artistic talent but also helped them overcome their fears and inhibitions, based on what she had learned about breaking free of her own fears of starting her business.

THE COST OF INACTION

As we witnessed in Dawn's story, there is a great cost to inaction, especially when it is our dreams or core capabilities that we aren't moving on. In Dawn's case it impacted her health. This is not uncommon. The energy we are holding back from taking action on our heart's desire is the energy that goes into overeating, drinking, and other habits that cause ill health. In my case the fear and anxiety associated with parasailing resulted in three sleepless nights and three days of experiencing distress rather than my relaxing vacation.

Sometimes the cost of inaction is less severe than losing our health. Inaction can result in *lethargy*. We simply don't have the energy to exercise, play a round of golf, or go out with friends. At work we don't have the energy to start the challenging project, call together a group of people to resolve a major breakdown, or let someone know they are creating a safety hazard that could cause a serious accident. And there is the cost that comes from this kind of inaction. It's the cost of regret for not taking an action to help someone, speaking up when you know better, or to saying no to a commitment you know you can't keep.

And this leads to the next cost of inaction: *mistrust*. When we don't act on decisions, commitments, and goals, others cannot possibly trust that our words will result in action. But worse, we stop trusting ourselves to keep our word. Our mistrust of ourselves is what keeps us from learning, from doing things differently to improve our quality, our communication, our relationships at home, and our health. Our very core *self-confidence* is eroded to the point where we are second-guessing our every step, our judgment, and our ability to achieve our dreams until we give up on ourselves.

With so many detrimental costs to inaction, why is it that we still find ourselves holding back, hesitating, and maintaining an unhealthy status quo or stuck position rather than taking the next step to free ourselves and move on to a greater level of success, happiness, and fulfillment?

FOUR OBSTACLES TO ACTION

There are four main obstacles to action: the need for comfort, fear, internal resistance, and perfectionism. The first step to overcoming them is to understand what they are and how each works to get in your way of achieving success.

Obstacle #1: Need for Comfort

Being comfortable is what keeps you in bed reading the paper on Sunday mornings when you don't have to go to work. Being comfortable is the feeling you have when you are talking with a friend who supports you. Being comfortable is when you are at work performing a routine job that you have done excellently a hundred times before without risk of failure. And these are all positive examples of being comfortable. However, when the need to feel comfortable drives your decisions and influences your level of cooperation, you can easily move into resistance. When you are asked to support a change, to learn a new skill, or to try something new, the feeling of discomfort surfaces. And if you aren't "safe" having uncomfortable feelings, you may do anything to avoid taking action—disappear, resist, rebel, or even attempt to blame the person who is the root cause for your discomfort.

Obstacle #2: Fear

Fear is the biggest obstacle to action, and in a sense it's also the basis for the other obstacles. Anytime you face the unknown or attempt an action that you've never accomplished before, fear enters the picture. The closer you get to your goals, the closer you get to your fear of failure *and* your fear of success. In either case, you are going to experience change—and change can be scary.

Laura worked as the HR director of a large computer manufacturer. She was given a project to implement a new compensation plan, and it was due in six months. She thought that was enough time and was quite relaxed about it. By the end of the third month, though, pressure was building, and she began to realize that the job was more complex than she had originally thought. She started having a queasy feeling in the pit of her stomach. And then, seemingly instantaneously, there was only one month left. The stress of the fast-approaching deadline was now enormous. She was frantically wondering how she could have been so stupid as to think six months was enough time. How could she get out of this mess? The fear was rising and getting in the way of her making things happen.

Fear is usually created through negative future fantasizing. You create in your own mind the tragedy that is about to happen and the impact on you or others when it does. Nothing has happened yet, but in your mind it is taking place right now. You can feel the pressure, the perspiration, and the panic. It can be as simple as the fear of showing up late to a meeting and hearing what others will say to you in their disappointment or as elaborate as the fear of not completing the project on time, being fired, not being able to find a job, and ending up homeless. You take the illusion as far out as your deepest internal fear.

To an outsider looking in, fear generally doesn't make sense. It almost never does. The fear is based on a future scenario that hasn't happened yet in which we have envisioned the worst case. John-Roger said it perfectly: "It's foolish to lose in your own fantasy." Yet we are constantly losing in our own fantasy when fear has taken over.

Obstacle #3: Internal Resistance

Internal resistance builds as you get closer to your goals. As you approach your desired outcome, you become aware of all of the work it will take to get there. At this point you realize that you can't just *talk* about the actions you're going to take someday in the future; you must actually *take* those actions.

The difference between the many physically gifted people who dream of playing professional football and those who actually go on to play in the pros lies in their behaviors. If you want to reach the level of athletic ability needed to play pro ball, there are many nonnegotiable behaviors you must adopt. Every step you take toward going pro involves more work. You need to train hard and get into peak condition before you can even try out for a team.

This can feel like prison, particularly if you make sacrifices for something that you have no guarantee of actually getting. The natural response is to resist. If you put in minimal effort, you will have lost nothing if you don't get what you're after. This same resistance shows up during change efforts, on major projects, and when having to conduct a difficult communication. In each case you are required to put in more effort, effectively plan your actions, and have the courage to begin without knowing the outcome. If you can overcome and do all that is required of you to reach your goal, the result is not imprisonment but the freedom that comes from accomplishing and living your dreams and achieving success at work.

Most of us have goals related to our careers and our families. If we don't continue to put the effort into achieving our goals by taking action, learning from our mistakes, and taking action again, we are giving up on ourselves. If we find *resistance* surfacing, it is important to ask questions to discover what the resistance is about. Is it fear of failure or fear of success? Is your goal still supporting your real intention and desire? Is there a skill that you are missing that is preventing you from going after your dreams? Do you need to just take action to get your energy started and move on your goal again? Do you need a coach or friend to assist you in staying on track until you become self-motivated again? You can ask questions about your beliefs, emotions, and behaviors to determine what needs changing and make the necessary adjustments.

Obstacle #4: Perfectionism

Perfectionism is the fourth obstacle to action. As you remember, the trap of perfectionism has been something to avoid all along the previous steps of the A-Loop, and it is essential to avoid when you are poised to take action. Too often we believe we must perform an action perfectly in order to succeed. If we can't be perfect, we do the one thing that dooms our efforts to failure: *We don't act.*

The trap of perfectionism keeps you in the planning phase forever. The problem is that when you are doing something for the first time, like planning a change effort or starting a new project bigger than any you have done before, you don't have the experience to know everything about it. You have to make judgment calls and learn from experience as it happens. Perfecting the plan before you take action only postpones the valuable lessons you will gain from experience. You see this in senior management teams who don't take action to clarify priorities. The default is that everything is a priority, which means nothing is a priority. Middle managers often want to say the right thing to their direct reports when implementing a change. So they fail to take action to communicate until negative rumors spread and result in resistance. And employees wait for the perfect direction given to them by their manager before they take action, causing delays, safety hazards, or breakdowns.

The truth is that taking action is not about perfection. This is a point that is often missed in business situations. Managers often believe that in order to succeed, everything must go like clockwork. So they spend inordinate amounts of time analyzing and planning and trying to take into account every possible factor in a project. One of two things happens: Either they never take action, or by the time they are finally ready to act, it's too late. For example, someone might lose an interesting ad campaign because he perfected it for so long that the client moved to an agency that could deliver faster. Or someone might be working on a presentation of the results of her medical research, but she takes so long to make the charts colorful and work her presentation to perfection that she arrives late to the meeting.

The ability to plan and execute anything flawlessly on the first try is a matter of sheer luck. And that is fine, because you're not aiming to be perfect. Your intention is to reach your goal, and you will soon see that there are proven ways to do exactly that.

TAKING ACTION EFFECTIVELY

There are six strategies you can use to support efficient action. We will spend the remainder of this chapter exploring how to jump into action and step away from fear.

First: Keep Your Eyes on Your Picture of Success

Before taking any action, be sure you understand why the action is important to you. What is the purpose being served? What accomplishment do you intend the action to achieve? Your Picture of Success is bigger than the action itself. In fact, the action is taken in service of a bigger sense of purpose and impact. While it may be uncomfortable or even scary to take action, in service to a larger Picture of Success you have the motivation to act anyway.

Paula, the promising employee, had spent her last three jobs making excuses and blaming others for her poor performance. And while she wanted to change this self-destructive behavior, she was scared to be vulnerable and admit weakness. However, her intention and Picture of Success clearly articulated her desire to be a top performer and to be respected by her peers and by upper management. Whenever Paula's fear of being vulnerable surfaced, she would use her Picture of Success to reinvigorate herself to give up control, be the "student," and admit mistakes.

It doesn't matter whether your Picture of Success is overcoming a fear of heights, accomplishing a project on time and on budget, or creating a long-term, meaningful relationship in which you can be married and live happily ever after; it means you may have to take actions that are uncomfortable or scary. Ride on the energy of your purpose to take you into areas you would normally avoid.

Second: Do Differently

Besides being necessary for accomplishing your goals, taking action is necessary for improving your results. When being indispensable is your desired result, continuous improvement is the game you are in—always. Sometimes it's massive change, while other times it is simple refinement. But in either case, it's not just any action that works.

Bill, the director of radiology at a medical center, made a recommendation to generate revenue by growing his department. When his proposal was turned down, he put together a second presentation composed of more PowerPoint slides demonstrating the financial efficacy of his proposal. His second proposal was "louder" but in essence was no different from his first one. The reason his proposals were rejected had nothing to do with his business case. That was sound. What wasn't sound was the fact there had been five grievances filed against his leadership by employees in his department. Morale was at an all-time low, and management wasn't going to approve expansion of his department given the risks associated with the employee-relations issues. Bill was requested to "do differently" by addressing his department's people issues through an engagement process. He listened to the challenges people faced and created accountable agreements for building trust and support. After six months of his leading differently, morale went up and grievances were resolved. He was now prepared and allowed to grow his department without the risk of internal breakdowns.

They key to effectively taking action is *doing differently*. This doesn't mean doing the same thing "louder," which leads arguments into complete polarization or leads to lots of activity with no results. Doing differently is finding a way—any way—to take a different action than you did the last time. When I coach executives or teams of people, my focus is always on "doing differently" to ensure that the actions being taken are new, more refined, more creative, and more aligned with their Picture of Success.

Third: Take Small Steps

Deborah, the struggling entrepreneur, picked up a client with her new purpose of helping entrepreneurs brand themselves to build business. It was a great assignment and Deborah was excited about supporting this person in building his business. She came back to her new client with a very comprehensive approach to building his business using branding as a foundation. Unfortunately, while the client liked the proposal and how complete it was, he wasn't moving forward by signing the contract. Realizing that her proposal might have been too big for her client, Deborah scaled back her service and offered only the initial five small steps to begin moving in the right direction to build the business. The new proposal was less costly, less time consuming, and, more important, more comfortable and less risky for the client. The client immediately agreed to the new proposal and they started the branding assignment.

When your stretches are too long and your actions too big, you can easily outrun your safety zone. Whatever you're doing begins to feel like punishment because the actions are too scary. The answer is to scale down your actions. Create smaller actions that eliminate some of the pain. You still need to stretch beyond your comfort zone, but not so much that you will be paralyzed.

Practice is another way to expand your safety zone. Did you use a kickboard when you learned to swim or training wheels when you learned to ride a bike? Kickboards support beginning swimmers so they can practice kicking their legs without having to worry about sinking below the surface. Training wheels allow the new cyclist to gain a sense of balance while having the confidence of reliable support. Essentially, the kickboard and training wheels enlarge the safety zone.

Small steps are like incremental weight training. You can build your action muscles one step at a time. With each small step you increase your knowledge and build trust in your own abilities. The stronger your muscles become, the more you can achieve with each new action you take. So break your actions down into small steps. Don't try to change everything at once. Go for small changes and let success breed success!

Fourth: Keep Moving

Movement is the key to success. It's by moving that you gain the experience to determine what works and doesn't work. You can have the best plans for moving forward, but until you implement and take action, they are just your theory about what will work toward achieving your goals. When we go into analysis paralysis in an attempt to make the "right" or "perfect" move, we end up stuck without the benefit of learning from experience.

Momentum brings successes we tend to take for granted. I can't drive by a KFC restaurant without thinking of the chain's colorful founder, the Colonel himself, Harland Sanders. At age sixty-five Sanders was forced into retirement when a new interstate highway bypassed his hotel and restaurant. After auctioning off the properties and paying the bills, his only income was a $105 monthly Social Security payment.

The one asset Sanders had left was a recipe for Kentucky Fried Chicken, and as unlikely as this sounds, he spent the next two years on the road trying to secure some additional income by selling the right to make his chicken to restaurateurs across the country. Sanders later claimed he was turned down *more than a thousand times* before he made a single sale. But he never quit moving toward his goal.

Five years after he started, two hundred restaurants were selling the Colonel's chicken. By 1964 more than six hundred restaurants had signed up. His retirement secured, Sanders sold his recipe and the franchise rights to a group of private investors for two million dollars. Four decades later, more than two billion of the Colonel's chicken dinners have been sold—and you can buy them in eighty-two different countries.

It is pretty obvious that the Colonel (it's an honorary title, by the way) knew the secret to overcoming internal resistance. And now so do you. Keep moving, because if you stop, there is no way you will ever succeed.

Fifth: Use Your Support Network

Drawing on others' support is critical to success. Just as you can influence other people to act through your own efforts, so too can they influence you.

It is no coincidence that institutions that force us to face our toughest challenges often feature built-in support. If you look at addiction-recovery programs such as Alcoholics Anonymous, you see that a major element is the use of *sponsors*: experienced members of AA who make themselves available on a face-to-face basis to new members. As new members struggle with their disease, they have someone to call on for advice and help. Often that call makes the difference between suppressing the need for a drink and falling off the wagon.

The entire multilevel marketing industry utilizes the concept of support networks. Each salesperson recruits, trains, and supports the next level of representatives. In return, the recruiting member earns a commission on the sales of people that he or she has supported.

Does it work? Mary Kay Ash built the world's second-largest direct seller of beauty products around the idea of ever-expanding levels of independent sales consultants supporting one another. Today there are more than one million sales representatives selling Mary Kay cosmetics. Amway was built on the same concept. Its parent company, Alticor, neared five billion dollars in annual sales, created by more than three million independent sales representatives who work for the consumer products direct marketer.

Without support, you are putting too much pressure on yourself to keep the ball rolling or to pick up the pieces when something breaks. Find people whom you can call on to encourage you, push you, and *egg* you on. Reach out for help when you can't believe you have any chance at ever reaching your goal. You'll be amazed at what one person's belief in you can help you do.

Finally—and Most Important: Have a Recovery Plan

You created a recovery plan in the chapter on forgiveness as the third part of effective delegation. And creating a recovery plan is also essential when you are taking action. You may think that if your plan of action is good enough, you don't need a recovery plan. But what your plan doesn't account for are the human errors that might occur, the unexpected breakdowns, and the unforeseen changes brought on by others that you depend on whether it is an upper manager changing priorities or a coworker you were depending on who calls in sick. When you have a recovery plan, a breakdown results in the implementation of "next steps" rather than the occurrence of the next crisis that causes paralysis, blame, and failure—to satisfy a customer, complete a project on schedule, or stay within budget. Recovery plans are key to achieve results from the actions you take.

THREE STEPS TO CREATING EFFECTIVE RECOVERY PLANS

Developing recovery plans is not difficult or arduous, even though it is rarely done. There are two essential steps to prepare your recovery plan and a third to initiate if you have to activate your recovery plan.

Step #1: Identification of Potential Breakdowns

It isn't necessary to anticipate every possible breakdown, only the major or different types of breakdowns. These might include conflicting priorities, a problem with a supplier, an equipment breakdown, or a faulty handoff between two people or functions. While you don't need to know exactly how and when the breakdown will occur, it is important to identify the different types of breakdowns in order to discuss alternative recovery plans.

In order to reduce costs, a medical center planned to consolidate two nursing units from the second floor and place them on the fourth floor. Administrators weren't sure it was going to work. The potential breakdown was that patient care would decline after the change. They set up a two-week measurement to track the impact of the change on patients.

Step #2: The Response

The response doesn't have to be the solution all figured out. Most of the time that won't be possible or necessary. The response simply answers the question "How will you mobilize your resources in order to resolve or respond to the obstacle to success?" For the medical center in the example above, the solution to the potential breakdown of poor patient care after the units' move was to convene the management team of the unit involved, along with the director of nursing, to move the units back to the second floor. In addition, the nursing unit that went back to the second floor developed a plan to resolve the issues causing the breakdown in patient satisfaction in order to quickly return to the fourth floor, where greater efficiencies could be actualized.

Step #3: The Follow-up (Once a Recovery Plan Is Initiated)

After convening the right people and developing a strategy for resolving or responding to the challenge, it is important to create a follow-up plan to ensure success. This follow-up plan is designed to fine-tune the solution to improve effectiveness, identify learning opportunities based on the challenge that surfaced, and provide recognition for the great effort people gave to resolve it.

Recovery plans tend to speed up changes and response times. In the case of the medical center, two weeks after the units moved, administrators discovered that patient care had declined in one of the units. Because they had a recovery plan, they were able to move the unit back to the second floor within three weeks. And then, based on the second part of the recovery plan, they convened the group to resolve the breakdowns associated with lower patient care. Within another two weeks, they had resolved the breakdowns and moved the unit back to the fourth floor, and this time there were no declines in patient satisfaction. From the time the move was first made, the problem was surfaced, responded to, and resolved within five weeks. And this included several different decisions made by various levels of leadership. Six months later, the medical center reported a reduction in cost, improved patient satisfaction, and improved employee morale based on the level of inclusion and the responsiveness of senior management.

ACHIEVING YOUR PICTURE OF SUCCESS—A REALITY

Taking action to be successful doesn't necessarily mean you will achieve success the first time around. Your actions may miss the mark, but follow the A-Loop by recommitting to your Picture of Success, recognizing that you are off track and taking ownership, and forgiving any judgments you have about being off track. Then self-examine to identify possible options, learn from your mistakes, and take action based on your learning to achieve your desired Picture of Success. That is the great news about the A-Loop. If you don't succeed the first time, you haven't lost. You are just a few more accountable steps from reaching your desired

Exercise: Take Action Now

Step 1: Clarify your actions

Based on your intentions, goals, and lessons learned from previous chapters, identify three actions you can take to move forward on accomplishing your dreams. Keep the actions small to ensure success.

Step 2: Solidify your commitment

For each action, commit to a start date and a target date for completion. Getting started is the most important step toward being successful.

Step 3: Identify your support system

Make a list of the people, environmental conditions, or tools that will support you in taking action. This could include a friend or coworker, playing music or lighting a candle in your office, or making sure you have canvases for painting.

Step 4: Create a recovery plan

Identify anything that could cause you to get off track. Maybe you get delayed in starting or you run into difficulties completing your first action. What will you do to recover and get back on track? What is your contingency plan? This is a key step in maintaining your momentum when obstacles are out of your control.

Step 5: Celebrate progress

Success is not determined only after you complete your goal. Recognize and celebrate success after each action you complete that moves you toward your goal and Picture of Success. Even if an action takes you off course, celebrate the learning you get from the experience. It is all preparation for achieving and sustaining success.

outcome. Over time your commitment to the A-Loop ensures your success and indispensability.

And you aren't complete yet. Once you are successful, anchoring your success to sustain it involves celebration—acknowledging yourself and others for the success you have attained. Keep reading to gain even more gratification from celebrating your success. Now the fun of success begins!

CHAPTER 11:
THE MISSING STEP— CELEBRATING SUCCESS

Taking action is the key to achieving results. Celebrating success is the key to sustaining success. It's what lets you know within yourself that you are on track, learning, improving, and making a difference. Unfortunately, some people believe celebration is a reason to stop striving, but this is fear-based thinking. Celebrating success provides encouragement, confidence, and inspiration to reach new levels of excellence. But celebration goes beyond having a party or getting a bonus. In this chapter you will explore meaningful and accountable ways to celebrate success.

"Success is getting what you want. Happiness is
liking what you get."

—H. Jackson Brown Jr.

Celebrating success goes beyond pats on the back, shaking
hands, or passing out trophies. Celebrating success is the
glue that holds excellence together. It is the thanks that
you express to yourself and others for contributions, effort, support, and guidance. It is the acknowledgment of learning, growth,
and improvement that you want to remember the next time—and
there is always a next time. It is the experience of awe and an
opportunity for deep humility—knowing that while you might
have put in a great effort, there were forces beyond you and the
people around you that made it possible for you to experience
success.

NEGLECTING CELEBRATION TAKES YOU
INTO THE VICTIM LOOP

There are so many reasons for not celebrating success. You don't
have time. You have to start on the next project. You're just doing
your job, so there's no reason to acknowledge your success. You
don't want to become lazy and give up striving for even greater
success. It wasn't a big enough success to warrant celebration—
there were even mistakes. While these all seem like valid reasons
for skipping the step of celebration, none of these excuses are good
ones. In fact, they represent a clear step into the Victim Loop.

Remember, the first two steps in the Victim Loop are *ignore*
and *deny*. And while people tend to ignore and deny mistakes they
make and problems that challenge them, they also ignore and deny
their success. As with any other time you visit the Victim Loop,
the longer you spend there the more it can become your automatic
response. You'll recognize that you are in the Victim Loop when
nothing is good enough, no matter how well you perform. You
actually feel dispensable, even though your performance might be
at a high level. But this mode of thinking is just a choice that you

can change at any time. If you aren't used to celebrating success and taking that action in a way that builds self-confidence and self-empowerment, follow the next steps to become an expert at effective celebration. Don't be surprised when the steps to celebrating success look familiar. You will be following the steps along the A-Loop as you celebrate success. Just as you would follow the loop to become more accountable in regard to a departmental problem or a breakdown within your team, you follow the exact same steps to become accountable for your success. While accountability is usually reserved for those times when mistakes are made, true accountability is also witnessed in success.

TAKING ACCOUNTABILITY FOR SUCCESS

It seems simple to take accountability for success. You may think that all you need to do is pat yourself on the back and say, "Nice job," But nothing could be further from the truth. Taking accountability for success means setting yourself and others up for even greater success. It comes with the responsibility to inspire, to teach, to prepare for future success, and to sustain current success. And this doesn't happen through a simple pat on the back. There are six steps for taking accountability for success.

1. Recognize your success

2. Own your success

3. Forgive the mistakes you made along the way

4. Self-assess your success

5. Learn from your success

6. Take action to celebrate

Identify a recent success you experienced and use that as an example to apply these steps. Have fun applying each step to experience celebration for your success.

Step #1: Recognize Your Success

First you have to realize that you have achieved your goal, accomplished your plan, or embodied your desired Picture of Success. This means that you actually take a breath before starting your next project to reflect on the "win" associated with your current accomplishment. And it doesn't have to be a perfect win for you to recognize success. Recognizing success doesn't mean just celebrating the results. It could also mean recognizing effective execution involving collaboration, decision making, execution, planning, or follow-through. It could be that you are recognizing improved performance, support from others, or overcoming a major challenge that threatened success.

Ultimately, recognizing success is simply expressing *gratitude*—giving thanks for all the supportive effort, guidance, participation, and problem solving that led to achievement, and even having gratitude for the "magic" that took place when a problem was solved or an action went more smoothly than expected.

Step #2: Own Your Success

It's not enough to just recognize success; it's important to own your part of the success. As we discussed earlier with respect to the step of ownership, there is no need to own it all, just your part. Maybe your part was leading the way, participating as a team member, or simply supporting the success as a temporary and part-time contributor. It is important to acknowledge the contribution you made to the success.

This is the step where you make sure that ownership extends to all stakeholders who were involved in the success. Regardless of their role and how much they were involved, it is important to acknowledge all of the *owners* who contributed to success.

Step #3: Forgive the Mistakes You Made Along the Way

Achieving success will almost always include imperfections and mistakes. Why? Because you are human and not perfect. It's from those mistakes that you have the opportunity to learn and grow.

But to reap the benefits of learning it is critical to forgive the mistakes and celebrate the wins, no matter how small or large. And if on the way to success you inconvenienced others, didn't communicate in a compassionate manner, or failed to support others, then taking ownership of those transgressions, asking for forgiveness, and making amends is also important.

Step #4: Self-Assess Your Success
Of course, there is a propensity to assess what might be done differently to improve results on the next implementation. Organizations have lessons-learned processes where they take considerable time analyzing and discussing alternatives for improvement. However, the value of success is often missed by focusing on the negative and not the positive. By not conducting an assessment to learn from your success, you miss out on an opportunity not only to celebrate but to learn. What worked well? What did you do differently that led to your success? What was better about your coordination, communication, teamwork, support, and execution that contributed most to your success? What was different about your attitude, behavior, and actions? Assessing your successes can be even more valuable than assessing your mistakes, since greater understanding can lead to other projects, goals, and assignments.

Step #5: Learn from Your Success
Self-assessment leads to learning, and there is nothing sweeter than learning from your success. Learning what specifically worked the best while you were accomplishing your goal, project, or assignment means that you will have a greater chance of repeating your success. You will be able to replicate the best of your efforts to accomplish your next goal.

I once worked with a department management team in a highly technical engineering organization. One of the managers, Joe, was having a challenge with his team and had spent the last three months of weekly meetings coming up with alternative solutions. Nothing had worked. After some prodding, he was convinced to share the challenging situation with the other department managers in their monthly meeting. Within three minutes, another department manager exclaimed, "We had that exact problem, and the only solution that worked for us was . . ." Joe couldn't believe it. All the effort and time he had spent trying to solve the problem hadn't worked, while his teammate's suggestion—in the form of sharing his own success—would solve the challenge within the next week.

Sharing successes is the fastest way to learn what works and spread the success throughout the organization. If that other manager had never taken the time to celebrate his own success in solving a problem, he never would have been able to recognize that Joe could solve his problem the same way. The solution might have been lost in his memory of all the tasks he has completed in the past. After Joe's experience, the organization set up a success-oriented lessons-learned process to augment its existing lessons-learned process, which focused on mistakes.

Step #6: Take Action to Celebrate

Once you have taken action to sustain your learning, you are ready to celebrate. What is the most meaningful celebration you can create for yourself? Is it a party or a quiet afternoon at the beach that makes you feel special? Maybe for you celebrating success means just taking a moment to review your success with a friend.

Another part of celebrating success is acknowledging those who supported you in achieving your success. This could mean throwing a party, calling a meeting to acknowledge others, or simply sending a note of thanks to all involved parties. While it is up to you to decide which kind of communication you will choose, your approach should not be determined by your needs alone. It should be based on the needs of the recipients of the communication and the reactions you desire from them. Do you want people to have a sense of pride, encouragement, inspiration, motivation, or gratitude? Each reaction can be strategized into the way you choose to celebrate success.

While celebration is important, it is critical to keep in mind that it is less about the reward and more about how you feel

Exercise: Celebrating Your Success

Celebrating Success

1. What are improvements or successes that you have made?

2. What can you do to celebrate your improvements or successes?

Understanding Your Preferred Style of Motivation

1. Are your needs more closely associated with being a self-starter or being an other-starter?

2. How do you like to be motivated on the job?

3. How are you typically motivated on the job?

4. What can you do differently to have a conversation about your motivational needs to gain greater satisfaction?

valued for your contribution. Ultimately, it's the value you feel that contributes to your sense of indispensability. This value comes from your appreciation of yourself, along with the appreciation others share with you for your contribution.

HAVE AN ATTITUDE OF GRATITUDE

> "Feeling gratitude and not expressing it is like wrapping a present and not giving it away."
>
> —William Arthur Ward

Be grateful you had what it took to succeed, and be thankful for the help you received in the process. Challenge yourself to find a reason to be thankful—for yourself and others. Maybe you had a creative idea. Maybe your kid cleaned up without your needing to beg. Maybe you completed a difficult project on time. Maybe your colleague landed a new account. Maybe you asked for help and allowed someone to contribute to your success. Or you made a healthy choice at lunch. Or you listened compassionately and made a great difference to a friend. Whatever it is you did, pat yourself or your teammates on the back. Start building your emotional bank account and theirs. Then the next time you have to tackle a big project or life challenge, you can draw on this wealth of inner support and acknowledgment. You will be more confident and trusting that you are able to accomplish the task at hand. And so will the people around you.

Celebrating is an essential part of success. You can't fully move on if you don't take a moment to acknowledge the road traveled. That is why movie crews have wrap parties: to complete, to close the loop of achievement, to allow them to conclude what just happened, and also to gear up for the next project.

Sadly, this step is often neglected. It is strange how we tend to be more familiar with the sense that we are not enough, that we should have done this better or faster. It is easier to see where we fell short than it is to see where we did a really good job.

RENEW YOUR INTENTION

Congratulations! You have successfully completed the A-Loop with celebration. Now you can move on to the final and never-ending step of creating your next intention. Choose what you are going to do next. Recommit. What is the next thing that matters to you? David Allen suggests keeping a running list that he calls "someday maybe." He recommends *capturing* what you want to accomplish, even if you are not yet ready to put any energy into it. Taking up golf, going back to school for your master's degree, learning sign language, starting a project to get better organized at work or at home, reading stories at a children's shelter, learning to play piano. When you are done with one project, you visit that list and choose your next adventure. That way, you accomplish not only what you have to but also what you *want* to. At the end of the day, the most important gift you can give yourself is to be indispensable to yourself.

The next and final chapter of this book provides you a review of the A-Loop to make it easier for you to repeat the process. Continue to learn, grow, and experience increasing success as you demonstrate indispensability.

CHAPTER 12:
LIVING AN INDISPENSABLE LIFE

As you have discovered by now, your life is a rich and colorful journey much like the rings of a rainbow. Each color is vibrant and distinct, but blends together with the other colors. Becoming indispensable has a clear pathway based on accountable action, but is filled with twists and turns that make any journey a rich experience. Sometimes, the surprises appear as roadblocks and challenges to overcome, while other surprises represent the grace of God or a gift from the universe. Either way, as you remain grateful for the entire experience the adventure is gratifying and fulfilling. And, there is more. Unlike most destinations, you haven't yet arrived. There are more wonderful journeys ahead. But, now there is a difference. You will be able to enjoy the remaining journey with the strength, confidence, and growth of having become more accountable and more indispensable. And that changes the quality of your experience. Now, the quest is about sustaining that growth and continuing on the path for even greater joy, abundance, and fulfillment. This chapter is about continuing to grow, building on your success, and enjoying life.

"My life is my message."

—Mahatma Gandhi

Congratulations! Becoming indispensable is nothing less than being the best you that you can be. Whether you have applied the A-Loop to your workplace or your home life, you now understand the personal gratification and joy that come from being of service to others—making a meaningful difference to those in your life. And most important, you have learned the fulfillment that comes from including yourself in the equation. Making yourself indispensable is not about accommodating others at your expense. It is about honoring yourself, your needs, and your dreams while you support others in being successful and living their dreams. And you have discovered that when others are successful and you were part of that success, your success grows as well. No one loses. Everyone wins.

You have also learned that becoming indispensable is not a path for the faint of heart. It takes courage and work to be accountable. Like the path of any great athlete, musician, or business leader, it comes with mistakes, miscalculations, bad decisions, unforeseen roadblocks, and an emotional roller-coaster ride that could cause anyone to stop and give up at any time. But you didn't. And it was worth it. For the lessons you have learned and the strength you have built can be applied for the rest of your life.

This chapter is about sustaining yourself as an accountable and indispensable person and reaching even greater heights of excellence and fulfillment.

INDISPENSABLE CHOICES

We learned in chapter 1 and applied when you *recognized your current reality* six choices that lead you to being indispensable. These choices continue to be important and evolve as you gain greater strength and influence with others. Let's review the six key choices for being indispensable:

1. Purpose driven

2. Play big

3. Adaptable

4. We centered

5. Priority focused

6. Value others

The first choice is being *purpose driven*. Chris, the plant manager, had a clear purpose that drove his learning and actions: to save his plant from failure. Deborah, the entrepreneur, had the purpose of assisting others in seeing their unique greatness and branding that to expand business opportunities. But she had to learn to see that in herself before she could help others.

What is your purpose as you see it today? How does it compare with the purpose that you had when you started reading this book? Has it changed? Generally your purpose will expand and change as your positive influence on others grows. Maybe it hasn't changed and you are still in process. Maybe your purpose has grown as you have seen even greater ways to make a difference and be of service in your organization or your family.

Your purpose can be approached in two ways: *play big* or play small. The choice to play big means you are showing up and being *seen* rather than hiding and trying to go unnoticed. You have the courage to take a stand, to take action rather than wait, and to disturb the comfort of mediocrity. Paula, the employee with potential, couldn't keep a job until she learned the difference between acting big and playing big. When she acted big, she worked hard at hiding her inadequacies and mistakes. When she played big, she had the courage to admit them, learn from them, and show up in her strength.

Being *adaptable* is critical to being indispensable. The world is changing way too fast to be stuck in a point of view or a habit of behavior that no longer works, or in an unhealthy relationship. Adapting to changes in technology and responding to the changing needs of others—whether they be your customers, your teammates, or your family—are critical for success.

You cannot accomplish your purpose and goals in a vacuum or without consideration of those around you. It is important to have a *we-centered* mind-set in order to include, engage, and support others around you. We are constantly interdependent with others, and any behavior, actions, or changes we make will impact others. Therefore, it is critical to being indispensable that we consider those chain reactions and engage others in surfacing the ripple effects of our decisions and actions. Paula discovered her impact on others as she failed to keep commitments and agreements. In her efforts to improve, she made the choice to act we centered by considering others rather than hiding from them.

It is easy to get lost in the many activities that can distract you during any given day. Whether it's Twitter, texting, chatting, or surfing the Internet, you have a multitude of distractions that didn't exist twenty years ago. And as organizations must accomplish more with fewer resources, management is tending to make everything a priority, which means little is completed or accomplished. Being indispensable means you have removed the distractions, regardless of their form, and have a clear sense of *priority*—what is most essential to moving you forward on your purpose and goals. Deborah had to learn that hard lesson to make her business successful. She had to stop avoiding the tough projects by attending pointless networking luncheons and put her attention, energy, and focus on building her business in meaningful ways.

Once you are clear on the priorities that will accomplish your purpose, you must effectively utilize the resources around you. The primary resources available involve thinking and energy. But you have to *value others* to take advantage of diverse thinking to solve problems and mobilize energy to take action once you have a solution. It is much easier to paddle a boat with four rowers than with one, but this requires the engagement of others. It is also the best way to sustain your energy; have others involved to do some of the heavy lifting. You can't leverage your valuable resources if you aren't utilizing all resources in your efforts to fulfill your purpose. Chris discovered that when he almost lost his plant and his position, due to going it alone and driving all the decisions himself. Until he embraced the concept of being *we centered* and included others in sharing ideas and making decisions, he was on a course of failure. Once Chris shifted to include his direct reports, the plant's performance improved and the plant was saved.

Finally, by continually choosing *accountable responses* you become indispensable. An accountable response requires owner-ship, action, and learning. And ultimately, through accountability you deliver results, which is the only way to manifest your purpose and dreams, demonstrate that you value others, and be perceived as indispensable.

What have you taken action on based on reading this book? What were the results? If the results were positive, then you achieved success for yourself and others. If your results weren't as positive, you learned from the experience, modified your approach, and took action again until you did achieve success. That is the path of being indispensable. Eventually you will be successful, and your success will benefit and include others.

NOT ALLOWING YOUR "HUMANNESS" TO STOP YOU

By now you have probably learned one of the most valuable les-sons for becoming indispensable—nothing can stop you except *you*! You can be slowed down and challenged by problems, mis-haps, and even tragedy, but as long as you are alive and continue making indispensable choices and demonstrating *accountability*, you will prevail. The only way to fail is to get stuck in the *Victim Loop*. If you are aware and open, you can even enter the Victim Loop and recover back to accountability. And given your human-ness, you will enter the Victim Loop from time to time—we all do. The best antidote for victimization is awareness and choice. Stay aware of the six phases of victimization including:

1. Ignore problems or the need to change

2. Deny your involvement

3. Blame others or yourself when there is a breakdown

4. Rationalize, justify, or defend your position to make others wrong

5. Resist changing, getting involved, or supporting others

6. Hide through business, crisis, or confusion

When any of these attitudes or behaviors show themselves, stop, turn around, and go in a new direction—turn immediately to accountability and follow the road map you have been guided through to get back on track toward being empowered, engaged, and making a difference. Otherwise you are left in the hopelessness, struggle, and suffering of the Victim Loop.

BACK ON TRACK—YOUR ROAD MAP OF ACCOUNTABILITY

No matter what journey you are on, there will be times when you get off the defined path to your destination. This could have a positive or negative result, but either way you are off course. However, it is not a problem if you have your road map in place to refer to. All you need to do is take out the road map and figure out where you are and what you need to do differently to get back on track. Simple. The *A-Loop* is the road map that I, along with thousands of others, have used to guide my journey to success and my path to becoming indispensable. And now you have experienced the A-Loop to make it your road map for achieving your goals, dreams, and aspirations. There are only seven steps to remember:

Step #1: Create a clear *intention* (Picture of Success)

Step #2: *Recognize* your current reality in reference to your intention

Step #3: Take *ownership* of improving it and making it better

Step #4: *Forgive* yourself and others for any mistakes or misjudgments

Step #5: *Self-examine* to explore both internal and external solutions

Step #6: *Learn* from your exploration and make choices for moving forward

Step #7: *Take action* to do differently in order to achieve success

Let's briefly walk through each of these important steps in the A-Loop—not only as a reminder of what you have learned but also to discuss additional learning. As we do so, reflect on your path of discovery and what you have learned about yourself as you traveled along this road map to success and indispensability.

Step #1: Intention

Creating *intention* is the key to accountability. It represents your Picture of Success—your destination. It is critical along the path to keep in mind where you are heading. Otherwise the challenges can overcome you. When I was learning to play drums and struggling to get the coordination of a drumroll, I almost gave up in frustration. The only thing that kept me going was my picture of playing in a professional group in front of thousands of people. Deborah, the entrepreneur, had to keep in mind her dream of using her unique gifts in branding to help people through all of the struggles she faced in her entrepreneurial business.

A key to being successful is sharing your Picture of Success, especially with those who are involved with supporting you to achieve it. Whether it is direct reports, teammates, or family members continually sharing, your Picture of Success becomes motivational for the actions they are taking to support you. If they have a larger sense of purpose, then they will overcome any frustrations or disappointments they may encounter. Also, as you achieve

your Picture of Success, sharing the updates with the people supporting you will give them the feeling of accomplishment.

What were your *intention* and Picture of Success that you created in chapter 4? Did you notice as you traveled the accountability path that your Picture of Success got clearer, bigger, and more
alive? This is very common as we move toward our vision. It will
expand and you will continue to see it in greater detail. This
doesn't necessarily mean your intention or Picture of Success has
changed. It only means that you are gaining a new level of understanding through your experience. It is the process of transform-
ing concept, theory, and dreams into reality.

Step #2: Recognizing Your Current Reality

Once you are clear about where you are going, you can *recognize
your current reality*. Where are you right now? What is working to
support your Picture of Success, and what isn't working? Keep in
mind that if something isn't working, that might not be because it
is broken. Maybe it served you well for where you were but won't
serve you in where you are going. Chris discovered this truth as
plant manager. He helped to make his plant successful through his
very directive style of leadership, in which he had the best answers
for improving the plant. But when the plant needed to move to a
higher level of excellence, he couldn't get there without involving
his people in a completely different way of finding solutions and
leading the actions taken. What is your current reality, and how
has it changed based on reading and applying the tools you have
learned in this book? Go back to chapter 1 and take the Indispensable Assessment again. Compare your scores and notice what has
changed. Remember to acknowledge any improvements or growth
you experienced. Notice what didn't change and use that as a reference point for continuing on the road map of accountability.

Step #3: Taking Ownership

Regardless of your current reality, *take ownership* of it and of
making it better. It is the only way to take dominion over problems

Key Insight #3: When Self-Assessment Scores Decline, It Could Be Good News

In over thirty years of working with individuals and teams conducting assessments, I have learned and witnessed an ironic truism. When scores go down, it could be because results are better. Why? It goes back to the idea that your Picture of Success will grow and expand as you take action to make it a reality. Your expectations also rise as you become more proficient. It's why you hear people say, "The more I know, the more I realize how much I still have to learn." It is not uncommon to witness an individual or team that has improved their performance substantially get lower scores on a self-assessment. This is because their standards have changed. They expect even greater levels of excellence than they imagined when they first generated their goal. It's actually quite motivating, but you have to discover the root cause of a declining score. Sometimes a declining score can reflect poor performance.

and regain your empowerment. No one can empower you except you, and taking ownership is the way to gain influence and self-confidence, even if you own a mistake. Otherwise the mistake, challenge, or problem is bigger than you. It's not making mistakes that makes you weak in the eyes of others. It is the lack of ownership of the mistake that makes you appear weak and vulnerable.

Paula, the promising employee, had great talent but came off as weak because she wouldn't own her mistakes. She completely lost her power to influence, to effectively communicate, and to get results because she wouldn't admit her failings and need to improve. Once she lost her job enough times, she learned to admit her failings, and from that point on, she regained her self-confidence and rebuilt the trust of others. True self-confidence comes not from perfect performance but from owning mistakes and doing something about them.

Step #4: Forgiveness

Since you are now taking ownership, it is critical to *forgive* yourself and others involved. Never forgiving keeps you stuck in the past. And as we have learned, driving forward means you have to stop looking in the rearview mirror or you will crash. How many of us have been plagued by past actions and self-judgments that keep us in a position of never being good enough? There is no way to be accountable and indispensable when you are stuck in that position. Freedom comes when you drop the judgments and focus on your intention, your purpose, your Picture of Success, and the road map of the Accountability Loop. The sooner you *forgive*, the more quickly you move on. The more slowly you forgive, the longer you are stuck in struggle and despair. Just as you want to own as much as possible, you also want to *forgive* it all.

What have you forgiven from your past that helped you to move forward in your life? What haven't you forgiven yet? Is it something you did or something someone else did? What is your fear of dropping that judgment right now and letting it go? What can you do differently to forgive them or yourself? What are you waiting for? . . . Do it now!

Step #5: Self-Examination to Discover New Solutions

After understanding your current state, taking ownership of any problems, and forgiving yourself and others for your current

Key Insight #4: Does Forgiveness Mean Forgetting?

I often hear individuals and groups say, "I can forgive, but I will never forget." There is a problem with this thinking. If you haven't forgotten the transgression, have you really forgiven, or are you still looking in the rearview mirror? Do you think you can move forward in your life always looking over your shoulder to the past? Yet we don't want to be taken advantage of again. To paraphrase a famous phrase, "Take advantage of me once—shame on you. Take advantage of me twice—shame on me."

The issue is not remembering or forgetting. The solution is *learning*. You want to learn from the past. That is truly valuable. Just because you don't forget the past doesn't mean you have learned. It's important to learn from failings, not to remember them.

situation, you are ready to begin *self-examination* to explore solutions. What can you do to change your attitude, mind-set, or behavior that will support you in resolving any roadblocks to your success? Using the best of your critical-thinking skills and tapping into the knowledge and experience of others are important for developing creative and practical solutions. After completing an internal and external exploration of solutions, you are ready to learn from this analysis.

Step #6: Learning

The previous step, self-examination, is about exploring opportunities and solutions in order to do things differently in the future. Self-examination always leads to *learning* if you are open to it. Being a *Master Learner* means that you use every opportunity for continued self-examination and learning. Learning could be a fine-tuning or a major transformation. Either way you are growing, developing new strengths, and gaining confidence.

The greatest lesson I have learned from others is that personal growth is like peeling away an onion. The good news is that it is a neverending discovery process that leads us to deeper understanding, greater compassion, and more openness. We trust ourselves more and can courageously expose our humanness with nothing to hide. The bad news is that we can fool ourselves into thinking, "This time I learned my lesson." The truth is that you probably did learn your lesson, but there may be a deeper form of the same issue that you will still need to learn later in life. When I learn a life lesson, I no longer say, "That will never happen again," referring to the mistake I made. I now say, "I'm grateful for that lesson," and wonder what my next lesson will be. . . . There's always a next lesson.

Learning is the key to becoming and staying indispensable, as long as you do something with your learning to make things better. Chris, Paula, and Deborah demonstrated their learning when they uncovered new mind-sets to adopt, new behaviors to exhibit, and new options for including others in their process of achieving success.

Step #7: Taking Action

Learning is great, but without putting your learning to use by *taking action*, you are simply repeating history. And if it's a history you don't like, you are creating more of what you don't want. Taking action is about doing things differently than you did before— hoping for a better result. But even if the result isn't better, you can learn from that and do differently again. And who knows? Maybe doing differently will have such a great impact that it will change your life forever. Deborah created the business of her dreams. Her work is her passion, and she attained financial success and reward! Chris changed his leadership approach forever and saved his plant from disaster. Paula finally developed a true sense of self-confidence rather than masking her insecurity by blaming others. Each of these people we followed through the stages of accountability made mistakes, showed personality flaws, and had a different style, but they all learned, took action, and reaped the rewards . . . not always immediately, but eventually.

What actions have you taken to be more accountable and to

Key Insight #5: When Inaction Is the Best Action

Too many people value action over results. They busy themselves with priorities, action plans, and things to do, fix, or change. When you are frantically rushing to get things done and you forget what it is you're trying to accomplish, it's time to slow down or even stop. Take a moment and breathe so you can figure out what is important to you. This is the time to go back to your intention, to self-examine what is driving you and who is the "master" of your activity. And based on what you learn from that process, you can either continue running and racing or choose a different course. Either way, you will know exactly why you are taking the present course— it won't be blind, automatic, uncontrolled behavior.

make yourself indispensable? What were the results? How did you not only help yourself but also have a positive impact on those around you—at work, at home, and elsewhere? What did you learn by taking action that will guide you in doing differently the next time? One thing you have learned through taking action is that there is no stopping you. You can take your lessons and actions to any endeavor you choose, any dream you have, and any accomplishment you want to manifest for yourself.

CELEBRATING PROGRESS AND SUCCESS

"You've come a long way, baby!" signifies the independence of women. It was one of my favorite commercials, and it applies to you right now—your independence. Ironically, you gain your independence not when you act in your own best interest but when you realize your interdependence and act in a way that serves both others and yourself. By following the road map of accountability and making choices that reflect your interdependence with others, you have not only changed your life for the better but also positively impacted many other people. It is important to acknowledge your success, at least inwardly if not outwardly. And if you are thinking, "It was nothing special to finish this book," think again.

You can *celebrate* that you didn't give up, even if you started and stopped many times in the process. You can acknowledge yourself for the exercises you did rather than focusing on the exercises you chose not to do. You can recognize each time you learned anything that caused you to change how you thought of yourself or others, how you communicated differently, or how you took action to make a difference. And even if you made no changes maybe you thought about the concepts and tools presented in this book. Even that is worth recognizing, because that could be the "seed" planted for a future harvest—a reference point for a future event in which the learning or application will unfold. Oh, there is plenty to acknowledge, to recognize, and to celebrate. Take a moment and give that gift to yourself. And don't forget the ultimate gratitude to express—that you gave yourself the time to care for yourself, make yourself even better, and make a more meaningful difference for others.

"NEXT!"—TAKING YOUR
INDISPENSABILITY TO THE NEXT LEVEL

Being indispensable is a never-ending pursuit of higher levels of
excellence and service to others. Sometimes after experiencing
success, it can be easy to say, "That's good enough." And while in
the moment you are right, it is good enough, there is always the
next level to move to. And that is when you use the magic word,
"Next!" After, and only after, celebration, you say, "Next," as a
reminder that you haven't arrived yet. Even if you achieved a goal
or attained a vision, as long as life isn't over, your quest to better
yourself is still in play.

Making yourself indispensable doesn't mean you have "arrived."
It only means that you have developed the inner strength and outer
ability to take on bigger challenges and help even more people. It
is very similar to building muscle. You can use weight lifting to
make yourself stronger, but what happens when you stop lifting
weights? The muscle atrophies. The same is true of indispensability. You may be indispensable for now, but if you stop growing,
stop caring for others, and stop being of value to those at work or
those in your personal life, you will make yourself dispensable all
over again.

One of the best ways to keep up your accountable behaviors
and indispensable choices is to help others become indispensable.
The greatest leaders are not those who achieved a business result.
The greatest leaders are those who helped other people become
great leaders who get great results. How can you be an advocate
for others to become great in their own right? How do you assist
others in discovering their unique value and taking accountability
for making themselves indispensable?

Can you have an organization in which everyone is indispensable? Yes, that is the highest-performing organization, with the
highest morale and the greatest ability to deal with adversity. It's

the organization you want to work for, contribute to, and create. Can you have a family in which everyone is indispensable? Yes, that is the family that is the most loving, caring, and supportive.

Develop your plan for sharing the keys presented in this book so that your team, your organization, and your family become more accountable, more trusting, more successful, and more fulfilling. Let it begin with you, and never let that flame within you burn out.

Thanks for your dedication, your courage, and your actions to make yourself indispensable and make your world a better place to live!

ACKNOWLEDGMENTS

First and foremost, I would like to give my deepest thanks to my wife, Kamin Bell, who not only taught me the meaningfulness of being indispensable but also was my greatest support system when I went through a period of my life where I felt dispensable. I am grateful for Kamin's demonstration of unconditional loving and empowering support.

This book would not have been written without several people who made it possible, and I give my deepest thanks to each and every one of them. Russell Bishop provided the encouragement to seek out a mainstream publisher and has been a guide and mentor to me for several years. Doe Coover, my agent, had the vision to gain the attention of mainstream publishers and provided great counsel along the way in the most caring and supportive manner imaginable. Jillian Gray, Julia Batavia, Allison McLean, Jamie Jelly, and the team at Penguin have been great mentors and coaches, providing excellent feedback and valuable insights in the writing of *Making Yourself Indispensable*.

Thanks to the contributions of others who provided feedback along the way. My support team included Sarah Samuel, Jane Grossman, Leslie Smith, Luis Manuel Ramirez, and Annette Shaked. Thank you for your valuable input.

I also appreciate many people who have guided me, taught me, and been way showers for me. I so appreciate the wisdom shared by Drs. Ron and Mary Hulnick, John Morton, John-Roger, David Covey, Paul Kaye, Sophie Chiche, Michael and Alisha Hayes, Stephan Mardyks, Michael Nila, Joerg Schmitz, Lawrence Caminite, David Rodgers, Craig Robbins, Tom Boyer, Teresa Edmondson, Barbara Thrasher, David and Kathryn Allen, Sally McGhee, and Davee Gunn.

Finally, this book represents the support and input of more people than I can name, representing my many clients, associates, friends, and staff. I especially want to thank Anthony Escamilla and Tom Hempelmann for their support behind the scenes at IMPAQ.

REFERENCES

Bishop, Russell. *Workarounds That Work*. McGraw-Hill, 2011.

Collins, Jim. *Good to Great*. HarperCollins, 2001.

Covey, Stephen M. R. *The Speed of Trust*. Free Press, 2006.

Covey, Stephen R. *The 8th Habit*. Free Press, 2004.

Godin, Seth. *Linchpin: Are You Indispensable?* Portfolio Penguin,
2010.

Halberstam, David. *Playing for Keeps*. Random House, 2000.

Hawkins, David R. *Power vs. Force*. Hay House, 2002.

Hulnick, H. Ronald, and Mary R. Hulnick. *Loyalty to Your Soul*.
Hay House, 2001.

Pink, Daniel H. *Drive*. Riverhead Books, 2009.

INDEX

accountability, 7, 35–37
  benefits of, 36–37
  defined, 43
  as life value and competency for success, 43–44
  myths about, 42–43
  Personal Accountability Model (*See* Personal Accountability Model)
  Picture of Success and (*See* Picture of Success)
  preparing for success, 47–49
  resistance to, 46–47
  for success, 191–92
Accountability Loop, 86–197, 203–10
  action to achieve success, taking (*See* action to achieve success, taking)
  forgiveness (*See* forgiveness)
  Master Learner, becoming (*See* Master Learner, becoming)
  ownership (*See* ownership)
  recognition of current reality (*See* recognition of current reality)
  self-examination to foster solutions (*See* self-examination to foster solutions)
accountable delegation and agreements
  obstacles, identifying, 122–23
  outcomes versus tasks, 121–22
  recovery plans and, 123

action to achieve success, taking, 170–88, 209–10
  benefits of, 172–74
  costs of inaction, 174–75
  doing differently and, 180–81
  exercise for, 187
  fear as obstacle to, 176–77
  inaction as best action, 209
  internal resistance to, 177–78
  moving forward and, 182–83
  need for comfort as obstacle to, 175–76
  obstacles to, 175–79
  perfectionism as obstacle to, 178–79
  Picture of Success and, 179–80
  purpose served by, 179–80
  recovery plans and, 184, 185–86
  small steps, taking, 181–82
  support networks, using, 183–84
activity focus, 30–32
Adaptable or Rigid choice, 26–28, 200
Allen, David, 196
Alticor, 184
Amway, 184
Anthony, Robert, 26
Ash, Mary Kay, 184
assistance of others, asking for, 94–96
awareness step, in learning, 155

Battle Hymn of the Tiger Mother
    (Chua), 12
Beatles, 72–73
behaviors, in self-examination, 149
beliefs
    in self-examination, 148
    of Victim Loop
        "I can't," 64–65
        "I'm right!", 64
        "It's not my style," 65
        "It's unfair," 64
Bishop, Russell, 105
blame phase of Victim Loop, 58–59
business trends, ownership of
        responding to, 110–11

Carroll, Lewis, 74
celebrating success, 189–97, 210–11
    accountability for, taking, 191–92
    exercise for, 195
    forgiving mistakes and, 192–93
    learning from success, 193–94
    neglecting to celebrate, effects of,
        190–91
    owning success, 192
    recognizing success, 192
    self-assessment in, 193
    taking actions for, 194–96
choices to become more indispensable,
        19–34, 199–202
    Adaptable or Rigid, 26–28, 200
    Play Big or Play Small, 24–26, 200
    Priority Focused or Activity
        Focused, 30–32, 201
    Purpose Driven or Goal Driven,
        21–24, 200
    Value Others or Disregard Others,
        32–34, 201–2
    We Centered or Me Centered,
        28–30, 200–1
choosing victimization, 54–55
Chua, Amy, 12
coaches, tips for finding, 97
Collins, Jim, 171
committing to making oneself
        indispensable, 9–40
    accountability and, 35–37
    behaviors necessary for, 15–18

choices to become more
        indispensable, 19–34
    examples of indispensable
        individuals, 13–14
    exercises for, 39–40
    faking indispensability trap, 11–13
    level of indispensability, 18–19
    "no one is indispensable rule,"
        breaking, 14
    victimization and dispensability,
        link between, 34–35
courageous heart, in facing current
        reality, 90–91
Covey, Stephen R., 22–23, 29
critical thinking
    cross-functional problem solving,
        145–48
    detail, 143
    digging deeper for answers, 148–49
    exercises
        for exploring automatic pilot
            responses, 150
        for improving critical thinking,
            147
    global view, 142–43
    integration, 144
    objectivity, 142
    perspective, 143
    problem-solving through, 144–45
    system-source link, 143–44
cross-functional problem solving,
        145–48
curiosity, 156–57
current reality, recognizing. *See*
        recognition of current
        reality

delegation and agreements. *See*
        accountable delegation
        and agreements
denial /blame trap, 113
denial phase of Victim Loop, 57
DePree, Max, 36
detail, 143
disappointment, 66
dispensable/dispensability, 3–5
    behaviors fostering, 4–5
    feeling dispensable, 3

making yourself dispensable, 3–5
    victimization and, 34–35
Disraeli, Benjamin, 149
disregarding others, 32–34
doing differently, 180–81
Drive (Pink), 22

Ed Sullivan Show, The (TV show), 73
*8th Habit: From Effectiveness to
    Greatness, The* (Covey), 22–23
Einstein, Albert, 83
emotions
    in self-examination, 149
    of Victim Loop, 65–66
        disappointment, 66
        guilt, 65
        mistrust, 66
        resentment, 66
engagement within organization,
    ownership of, 110
entitlement, in faking indispensability,
    12–13

Facebook, 23
fake indispensability, 11–13
    entitlement and, 12–13
    power and force and, 11–12
fear
    of blame, 46
    of failure, 47
    as obstacle to taking action, 176–77
    of success, 47
FedEx, 101–2
feeling stuck, 51–54
force, in faking indispensability,
    11–12
Ford, Henry, 64
forgiveness, 117–36, 206–7
    accountable delegation and
        agreements, 121–23
    celebrating success and, 192–93
    as core competency, 130–31
    exercise for, 136
    firings and, 129–30
    holding others accountable, 124–29
    human factor and, 118–19
    measure of accountability and,
        119–20

process of, 134–35
    saying "I'm sorry" doesn't mean,
        120–21
    self-forgiveness, 132–34
    strength to forgive, developing,
        131–32
    universality of, 132
Fortune, 89
fulfillment, from being purpose
    driven, 24

Gandhi, Mahatma, 13, 44
Get Better or Get Beaten! (Slater),
    89–90
Giving Sorrow Words (Lightner),
    114
global view, 142–43
goals
    purpose behind, 21–24
    setting, 73–76
Godin, Seth, 7
Good to Great (Collins), 171
gossip, 124–25
gratitude, expressing, 33
guilt, 65

Habitat for Humanity, 74
Halberstram, David, 95
Hawkins, David R., 11
hiding phase of Victim Loop, 61–62
holding others accountable,
    124–29
    acknowledging situation without
        judgment, 127
    gossip trap, 124–25
    ignoring trap, 125
    perseverance, 128–29
    recommitment and, 128
    recovery plans and, 128
    rescue trap, 125–26
    reviewing commitment or
        agreement, 126–27
    steps for, 126–29
    supporting person, 127–28
    traps in, 124–26
Huffington, Arianna, 23
Huffington Post, 23
Hulnick, Mary, 133

Hulnick, Ron, 133
human factor, and forgiveness,
    118–19

"I can do this myself" trap,
    157–58
"I can't" belief, 64–65
ignoring broken commitments or
    agreements trap, 125
ignoring problem phase of Victim
    Loop, 56–57
IMPAQ, 102
"I'm right!" belief, 64
inaction, 209
indispensable, making oneself,
    5, 6–8
  accountability and (See
    accountability)
  committing to (See committing
    to making oneself
    indispensable)
  living an indispensable life (See
    living an indispensable life)
  as process, 5
  road map for, 6–8, 41–49
inner listening, 161–67
integration, 144
intention, 69–85, 204–5
  exercises
    for clarifying intention, 77
    for keeping intention alive, 84
  mind-set for high performance,
    73–82
  perfectionism and, 71–72, 73
  picturing and testing success
    (See Picture of Success)
  reverse engineering, 83–85
  risk taking and, 72–73
  stating intentions and setting goals,
    73–76
internal resistance to taking action,
    177–78
"It's not my style" excuse, 65
"It's not the way we do things around
    here" trap, 158–59
"It's unfair" mind-set, 64
"It wasn't invented here" trap,
    159–60

Japanese earthquake and tsunami, 30
Jobs, Steve, 44
Johnson, Earvin "Magic," 13, 74
Jordan, Michael, 44, 95–96,
    118, 120
jumping to solutions trap, 138–39

Kan, Naoto, 30
Kentucky Fried Chicken, 182–83
King, Martin Luther, Jr., 13, 44

Lao-tzu, 167
Leadership Is an Art (DePree), 36
learning
  Master Learner, becoming (See
    Master Learner, becoming)
  from success, 193–94
lethargy, 175
Lightner, Candy, 114
Lightner, Cari, 114
Linchpin: Are You Indispensable
    (Godin), 7
Lincoln, Abraham, 13, 72
living an indispensable life, 198–212
  accountable responses and, 202
  awareness of victimization and,
    202–3
  celebrating success and, 210–11
  choices for, 199–202
  road map of accountability and,
    203–10
Loyalty to Your Soul (Hulnick &
    Hulnick), 133

Madoff, Bernie, 22
Mandela, Nelson, 7, 13
martyrdom trap, 112–13
Mary Kay Cosmetics, 184
Master Learner, becoming, 152–69,
    208–9
  awareness of role in problem, 155
  barriers to, 154–55
  curiosity and, 156–57
  exercises
    for exploring teacher and learner
      relationships, 163
    for integrating discoveries, 168
  inner listening and, 161–67

motivation and, 156
steps to, 155–56
teacher and student roles in,
    161–62, 163
traps that prevent, 157–60
understanding and, 155–56
me centered, 28–30
micromovements, 38
mistrust
  as cost of not taking action,
    175
  Victim Loop and, 66
Mothers Against Drunk
    Driving (MADD),
    114
Mother Teresa, 13
motivation, in learning, 156
moving forward, 182–83

neutral frame of mind, in
    facing current reality,
    89–90
Nicklaus Jack, 84
"no one is indispensable rule,"
    breaking, 14

objectivity, 142
obstacles, identifying, 122–23
out of control, feeling, 3
ownership, 99–116, 205–6
  empowerment as reward of taking,
    99, 115–16
  exercise for, 115
  100% ownership in projects,
    taking, 104–6
  problems with avoiding, 100–1
  shared, 101–2
  of success, 192
  taking your power back through,
    101–4
  during transition, 113–16
  traps to beware of, 112–13
  at work, 106–12

perfectionism
  as obstacle to taking action,
    178–79
  paralysis created by, 71–72, 73

Personal Accountability Model, 2–3,
    44–46, 203–10
  Accountability Loop
    (See Accountability Loop)
  intention (See intention)
  Victim Loop (See Victim Loop)
perspective, 143
Picture of Success, 44, 70–71, 76–82,
    204–5
  comparison of different, 82
  creating, 77–79
  exercises
    for creating picture of success, 79
    for keeping picture of success
      alive, 84
  questions for developing, 77
  taking action and, 179–80
  testing, 79–82
Pink, Daniel H., 22
Play Big or Play Small choice,
    24–26, 200
Playing for Keeps (Halberstram), 95
power and force, in faking
    indispensability, 11–12
power trap, 112
Power vs. Force: The Hidden
    Determinants of Human
    Behavior (Hawkins), 11
prioritization, 31–32
  of current reality, 93–94
  ownership of staying focused on
    priorities, 109–10
Priority Focused or Activity Focused
    choice, 30–32, 201
proactive recovery plans. See recovery
    plans
projects, taking 100% ownership in,
    104–6
"Prove it to me" trap, 160
Purpose Driven or Goal Driven
    choice, 21–24, 200

rationalization phase of Victim Loop,
    59–60
recognition of current reality,
    86–98, 205
  assistance, asking for, 94–96
  coaches, tips for finding, 97

recognition of current reality (*cont.*)
  comprehensive review of current
      reality, 91–93
  courageous heart, 90–91
  finding right coach, tips for, 97
  identifying current reality, 87–88
  neutral frame of mind, 89–90
  prioritizing current reality, 93–94
  success, recognizing, 96–98
recovery plans
  delegation and, 123
  development of, 185–86
  follow-up plans, creating, 186
  holding others accountable and, 128
  identifying potential breakdowns as
      step in developing, 185
  response to potential breakdowns,
      formulating, 185
  taking action and, 184, 185–86
renewing intention, 196–97
rescue trap, 125–26
resentment, 66
resistance phase of Victim Loop, 60–61
reverse engineering, 83–85
rigidity, 26–28
risk taking, 72–73
road map for becoming indispensable,
      6–8, 41–49

safe work environment, ownership of
      creating, 112
Sanders, Harland, 182–83
school of hard knocks, 154–55
Schwab, Charles, 149
self-assessment, 206
  in celebrating success, 193
self-esteem, 12
self-examination to foster solutions,
      137–51, 207–8
  critical thinking and, 142–45
  exercise for getting unstuck, 141
  jumping to solutions trap,
      138–39
  narrow view of accountability as
      limiting, 140–42
  questioning, importance of,
      139–40
self-forgiveness, 132–34

shared ownership, 101–2
silo behavior, 5
  ownership of breaking down, 109
Slater, Robert, 89–90
Smith, Dean, 95
Smith, Frederick W., 101–2
Speed of Trust, The (Covey), 29
Steinem, Gloria, 162
success
  celebrating (*See* celebrating success)
  fear of, 47
  Picture of Success (*See* Picture of
      Success)
  preparing for, 47–49
  recognizing, 96–98
  taking action to achieve (*See* action
      to achieve success, taking)
support networks, 183–84
system-source link, 143–44

taking action
  to achieve success (*See* action to
      achieve success, taking)
  to celebrate success, 194–96
transition, ownership during,
      113–16

understanding step, in learning,
      155–56
Updike, John, 71
us versus them mentality, 29

Value Others or Disregard Others
      choice, 32–34, 201–2
Vélez, Álvaro Uribe, 13
victimization
  awareness and choice as antidote
      for, 202–3
  dispensability and, 34–35
  Victim Loop (*See* Victim Loop)
Victim Loop, 50–68
  beliefs of, 63–65
  blame phase, 58–59
  choosing victimization, 54–55
  denial phase, 57
  as downward spiral, 62–63
  emotions of, 65–66
  examples of victimization, 52–54

exercise for getting past
    victimization, 67
feeling stuck as sign of being in,
    51–54
hiding phase, 61–62
ignoring problem phase, 56–57
overcoming, 67–69
phases of, 55–62
rationalization phase, 59–60
resistance phase, 60–61

Ward, William Arthur, 195
We Centered or Me Centered choice,
    28–30, 200–1
Welch, Jack, 89
Wheel of Indispensability, 9–10, 20
    choices to become more
        indispensable and (See choices
        to become more indispensable)
Williams, Robin, 115
Williams, Roy, 95–96

Winfrey, Oprah, 7, 13, 44
Wonder, Stevie, 115
work, ownership at, 106–12
    business trends, of responding to,
        110–11
    of engagement within organization,
        110
    exercise for increasing, 111
    in meetings, 106–8
    priorities, of staying focused on,
        109–10
    safe work environment, of
        creating, 112
    silos, of breaking down, 109
    of surfacing issues, 108–9
    of unresolved issues, 108–9
Workarounds That Work
    (Bishop), 105

Zagat, 74
Zuckerberg, Mark, 23

3 Start Today!
EASY STEPS
increase your success, confidence & impact.

1 Get the FREE Missing Chapter
Making Yourself Indispensable was originally over 300 pages. You can find the missing chapter online with assessments, activities and tools to help you become more indispensable. Download FREE at:

www.MarkSamuel.com/chapter

2 Be Part of the Indispensable Community
Learn strategies, tools and "tricks" of Making Yourself Indispensable and living in the "A-Loop" with FREE Newsletters, Podcasts, Special Webinars shared by Mark Samuel. In addition, get connected with other "A-Players" who are dedicated to making a meaningful difference for improving their workplace, their community and the world at large. This is an exciting opportunity to get exclusive content and expand your network of people who think like you and are making a positive difference. Sign up at:

www.MarkSamuel.com/community
Follow us on Facebook > Linkedin > Google+

3 Making Yourself Indispensable Guidebook
This step-by-step guide walks you through each step of the "A-Loop" with activities to Make Yourself Indispensable at work and in your personal life. Mark Samuel guides you through each step helping you prepare your Mindset, Attitude and Critical Thinking Skills to take actions which will improve your success, expand your influence, and refine your communication skills to add value in the workplace and at home. You will not only become more indispensable at work but also with your most important relationships in your personal life. For more information go to

www.MarkSamuel.com

Making Yourself
INDISPENSABLE

This interactive, energizing & informative WORKSHOP promises to provide you the experience, activities and practical steps to increase your indispensability.

Benefits

- Increase your positive influence and respect
- Reduce the stress from too many priorities and not enough time
- Enhance trust in your most important relationships
- Devise a clear road map to your next promotion
- Experience the fulfillment of a more supportive relationships with your family
- Achieve higher levels of performance and success
- Receive higher levels of recognition for your valuable contribution

What You Will Learn

- Creating a powerful Picture of Success to guide your future
- Identifying a practical strategy for overcoming "bad" habits that has undermined your success
- A method for accessing your power when you need it the most
- Keys for improving relationships and conducting difficult conversations
- A process for expanding your network of other "A-Players" to create your own virtual "A-Team"
- A follow-up system to keep you on track for sustaining results

To sign-up visit www.MarkSamuel.com/workshop

Rapid
TEAM RESULTS

This unique Team Accountability Process guarantees measurable results within 3 to 6 months! Based on 25 years of experience and measurable data, Rapid Team Results improves the 3 critical factors in team success: Team Execution, Team Relationships and Achieving Deliverables. In one day, the team develops a new mindset and habits of execution to achieve a new standard of excellence that will be realized within 3 to 6 months.

Team Results

- Increase team execution between 60% and 80%

- Improve team relationships between 15% and 35% including Trust, Support, Communication, and effectively Managing Conflict

- Increase the number of projects that are achieved on schedule, on budget and meeting expectations

- Breakdown silos, blame, and competing priorities

Outputs from Rapid Team Results

- A team "Picture of Success"

- 15 to 25 Habits of Execution to increase high performance

- Baseline measurements to assess execution effectiveness

- 3 to 5 Improvement Goals and Action Plans for improving execution

- Assessment of Team Relationships in 15 areas related to team performance

- 1 to 3 Team Agreements for improving team relationships

- Identify key deliverables that will be achieved for demonstrating success

For more information: Go to IMPAQ's Website at www.impaqcorp.com